BRINGING THEOLOGY TO LIFE

Key Doctrines for Christian Faith and Mission

DARREN C. MARKS

IVP Academic

An imprint of InterVarsity Press
Downers Grove, Illinois

InterVarsity Press
P.O. Box 1400, Downers Grove, IL 60515-1426
World Wide Web: www.ivpress.com
E-mail: email@ivpress.com

*InterVarsity Press® is the book-publishing division of InterVarsity Christian Fellowship/USA®, a movement of
students and faculty active on campus at hundreds of universities, colleges and schools of nursing in the United States
of America, and a member movement of the International Fellowship of Evangelical Students. For information
about local and regional activities, write Public Relations Dept., InterVarsity Christian Fellowship/USA, 6400
Schroeder Rd., P.O. Box 7895, Madison, WI 53707-7895, or visit the IVCF website at <www.intervarsity.org>.*

All Scripture quotations, unless otherwise indicated, are taken from the Holy Bible, New International Version®.
*NIV®. Copyright ©1973, 1978, 1984 by International Bible Society. Used by permission of Zondervan Publishing
House. All rights reserved.*

Design: Cindy Kiple
Images: Lisa Spindler/Getty Images

ISBN 978-0-8308-3852-3

Printed in the United States of America ∞

Library of Congress Cataloging-in-Publication Data

Marks, Darren C.

   *Bringing theology to life: key Christian doctrines for Christian
   faith and mission / Darren C. Marks.*
     p. cm.
   Includes bibliographical references and indexes.
   ISBN 978-0-8308-3852-3 (pbk.: alk. paper)
   1. Theology, Doctrinal. I. Title.
   BT75.3.M325 2009
   230—dc22

                                                        2009011755

P	20	19	18	17	16	15	14	13	12	11	10	9	8	7	6	5	4	3	2	1
Y	26	25	24	23	22	21	20	19	18	17	16	15	14	13	12	11	10	09		

For Pia, Gareth and Beatrice.

Without them, everything I write would be mere theory.

CONTENTS

INTRODUCTION

It must be said from the outset that this is not a *dogmatic* or *systematic* theology in the classical sense. While there is much systematic theology in the following pages, it really is a primer on the necessary theological ideas that every Christian should be familiar with in order to live and serve the gospel fully. Certainly there are some major gaps (e.g., the doctrine of creation), which does not mean these subjects are unimportant. Some ideas simply couldn't be adequately expressed given the space limitations of this book.

The structure of this book is simple: I begin with God, then move to the problem of humanity before God, God's remedy in Jesus Christ, how Christians *know* that remedy now in the Spirit, how the Spirit uses the Bible and sacraments to lead Christians into a kingdom mentality, what exactly that kingdom is, and finally what it means to be a kingdom people. In short, we will discuss God, sin, the incarnation, the Spirit, the Bible and sacraments, heaven, and finally the church.

Many Christians are not aware that the church *now* lives in heaven and of what role God's Spirit plays in making that present and future truth real. Some traditions, particularly evangelical and Pentecostal, tacitly understand that a Christian moves from the kingdom of the world to God's kingdom (heaven), but even in those traditions heaven is often understood as a far-off reality and something to be worked toward or anticipated. I also want people to understand that ethics—how Christians live in grace—is firmly built on the nature of God, God's love in Christ, God's present activity and God's people as reflections of that powerful loving God.

PURPOSES AND CONVICTIONS

This book is written with two purposes and two convictions in mind. First, I believe that theology, or rather *academic* theology, is largely divorced from the needs and concerns of members of the community of faith. Academic theology is taught in the abstract, as if it has no bearing on parish or community life. Instead, it presents challenges or problems that specialists write about for the other specialists in their field. Any intersection between the academy and community is left to hapless theology students.

I don't believe this is the intent of most academic theologians. Most theology is indeed offered as service to God by theologians, and thus the disconnect is both unfortunate and unnecessary. The lack of intersection between the life of parish and Christian theology short circuits effective Christian mission. I hope in some small measure to redress that imbalance by clarifying that Christian theology is exactly the content of the life of the Christian community in terms of its worship and therefore its understanding of God in Christ. My method is simple: I introduce the church to the insights of academic theologians. What we together have to say is the result of a fundamental desire to serve the church by loving God with all of our heart and mind.

Second, theology is a recounting of the *whole* drama of redemption. To skip a chapter is to miss the story. Thus the chapters of this book are thematic *and* interwoven. Though they are not the last word on the subject, they are sufficient to tell the story well. Hopefully they will move Christians to ponder more deeply the incomprehensible love of God in Christ as well as the Christian witness to that astounding promise.

In order to accomplish these two purposes, I have avoided citing too many events and theologians; and I have limited the use of footnotes and theological jargon. Above all, I see this book as an act of worship, a story of several important theological ideas that cement confidence in the Christian life and its Lord. In writing this book I hoped to rediscover the kind of theology that first captivated me. I was drawn to theology not because of the wonderful logic or castles of the mind it offered as the queen of the sciences, but because when I read Martin Luther or Karl Barth my heart swelled. When I read my Bible, I found that their lips moved with the Bible. Thus this book gave me an opportunity to use the Bible in a manner unusual for academic theologians. Here, I too try to move my lips to the Bible in order to allow God to speak.

The conviction with which I write is also twofold. I am not particularly attached to any single tradition, denomination or account of the Christian life, but I have felt wonderfully free to learn from all. Certainly, there are places at which I have felt more at home, and certain voices resonate more deeply with me, but I count it a grand blessing that I am more than the sum of my own parts theologically, and I try to be generous in roaming the theological family tree in discussions.

Two of my great *doktorvaters* (doctoral fathers) at Oxford and Bonn often joked that I was neither Lutheran enough for the one nor Reformed enough for the other. A third was an evangelical Anglican who was bemused at the extremes I felt. Further, my closest theological friends at Oxford were a Jesuit, a Dominican and a Franciscan. I count myself fortunate to have learned from all and continue this process in my interest in global theology and mission activity. I am convinced that speaking with other Christians, even those we might find suspicious, is an imperative for us, and I invite you to journey with me in this work. Of course, I have also journeyed with many other Christians through their writings, and each has been a wonderful companion in his or her own way. Reading the Bible with other saints is a wonderful gift from God.

I often remind my students of the words of Karl Barth in the opening of his book on nineteenth-century European theology. Barth, despite profoundly disagreeing with most of nineteenth-century European theology, reminded his readers that "God is the Lord of the

Church. He is also the Lord of theology. We cannot anticipate which of our fellow-workers . . . are welcome in our work and which are not. . . . We are *with* them in the Church."[1] This book views contemporary theologians as fellow workers, whose goal as modern academic and ecumenical theologians is to better understand their Christian mission and to assist the church in finding its theological mission. Sometimes we might disagree, even profoundly, but we, as Barth indicates, are *with* them in the church of God.

I invite you to sit with me in the academy and to learn how theologians try to be faithful in their understanding of the gospel. I take their ideas and offer them as fuel, sustenance and even hope to the church, even though at times we may disagree. But in that disagreement we too might be sharpened, perhaps learning new ways of thinking about God. (I encourage those are interested in the relationship between theological scholarship and the mission of theologians to look at two of my books—*Shaping a Theological Mind* and *Shaping a Global Theological Mind*.)

The other conviction I have is not mine alone: Western Christianity has a great problem that Christian minds and hearts must address. We have turned theology and Christianity into a kind of self-dialogue in which we believe we think *sicut Deus* (just as God). There is no humility, no Christian supplication in this, and it has produced a church without much power. This underlies the extensive dialogues with modernity in this book. Through greater understanding of our culture and its origins, the church can differentiate itself from it and enhance its mission therein.

OVERVIEW

The theo-logic of the text begins with the doctrine of the *Trinity*. I believe that an understanding of the Trinity is essential for Christian confidence in God. Further, the Trinity is also a promise of love and

---

[1]Karl Barth, *Protestant Theology in the Nineteenth Century,* trans. Brian Cozens and John Bowden, ed. Colin Gunton (Grand Rapids: Eerdmans, 2002), p. 3.

presence for Christian worship and life. The Trinity is the Christian reflection of its worship of the Lord.

Chapter two deals with the doctrine of *sin*, arguing that to understand sin properly is to understand who Christ is and what God has done in Christ. Rather than a message of pessimistic oppression, understanding sin in light of Easter means that Christians can actually live as redeemed people, because sin and the enemies of God are defeated (see Rom 5).

Chapter three ties together the two previous chapters by looking at the meaning of the *incarnation* as God's love letter to humanity. Jesus Christ is not only God incarnate, the redeemer of humanity, but he is also the promise of God to be humanity's God despite persistent human folly. This means that we can become creation-embracing children of God because of God's validation of creation, human destiny and humanity as God's creatures (see Phil 2).

The doctrine of the *Holy Spirit* is the subject of the fourth chapter. In this chapter I argue that God's sanctifying work enables us to live as Christ's followers (action) and to be witnesses to God's grace in Christ (speech). The transformation of our lives through the power of the Spirit is the basis of Christian ethics and communities of change (Gal 5).

Chapter five examines how Christ is present to the church in the Spirit by the mediating graces of the *Bible* as the Word of God and the *sacraments* as the presence of God. Taking a via media between highly sacramental and nonsacramental theology, I argue that the Scripture and sacraments are vehicles in which Christ is really present and through which sin is overcome in the life of the Christian. Word and sacrament are witnesses to that reality of God which declares, redeems and sustains us for life before and in worship of God (2 Tim 4:1-5). Ordinarily, these topics are covered in the doctrine of the church (ecclesiology) because the church is where the Bible and sacraments are normally heard and received. I distinguish them because I want to stress that they are the means for Christians to understand (1) their hope in Christ (heaven) and (2) the church as the place in which that hope and reality is now in motion.

Chapter six focuses on *heaven*, arguing that through Christ's victory and the Spirit's presence with the community of faith, the triune God has inaugurated the kingdom of God in our midst. As Christians faithfully appropriate the promise that all things are presently under Christ, their hope in heaven is actualized. Heaven, in other words, is *here* in the church and in God's activity in all the places the church witnesses to Christ. This understanding of heaven fuels Christian presence and mission in the world because no person, place or culture is Godforsaken (1 Pet 3:15-16).

Chapter seven casts a vision of the *church*, the family or community of God, as united by common vision and mission despite the external forms it might embrace. I return to the ancient creedal formulation of "one holy catholic and apostolic church" by exploring how each of the previous chapters argues for intra-Christian ecumenicity (2 Cor 4).

For those who wish to move further in discussion, I have provided discussion questions and a broad bibliography at the end of each chapter. I encourage you to read these wonderful books and to engage in discussion with others to clarify and deepen understanding of the topic at hand.

1

THE DOCTRINE OF
THE TRINITY

*"Therefore go and make disciples of all nations, baptizing them in
the name of the Father and of the Son and of the Holy Spirit."*

MATTHEW 28:19

IS THE DOCTRINE OF THE TRINITY IMPORTANT? Yes. The Trinity
is the *specifically* Christian understanding of God. Christians worship a
God who is uniquely self-revealed as Father, Son and Holy Spirit. The
Christian God *is* a Trinity. However, the Trinity has fallen on hard
times over the last few centuries of Western Christianity. At best, it has
been relegated to an incomprehensible, abstract and useless mystery. At
worst the Trinity is viewed as an invented theological teaching used to
keep a hierarchal male-centered system in power. Certainly, the Trinity
is a mystery; it is not a truth we come to without the aid of revelation.
However, the claim that the Trinity was invented to support a male
hierarchy is quite false.

How did Christians come to embrace the trinitarian understanding
of God? In their worship of Jesus of Nazareth as God's promised Messiah, the earliest Christians realized and experienced several important
things. First, after Jesus' resurrection from the dead and ascension into

heaven, they realized that Jesus of Nazareth was not simply an important person or role model. Jesus did and promised things that properly belonged to God alone. Further, early followers of Jesus of Nazareth worshiped him as Lord and Savior. These radical claims apparently contradicted Jewish monotheism. Monotheism for Jews meant *one* God who alone was Creator of the world, Redeemer of God's people and Sustainer of the entire cosmos. There was only one Lord, one Savior and divine Presence worthy of being worshiped. There wasn't two and certainly not three gods who fit this job description. Jewish monotheism left three options for the earliest Christians.

Potentially, Christians could agree that they were not monotheists, that Christianity believed in three gods: Father, Son and Spirit. Indeed, this option created two offshoots that early Christian theologians and communities had to contend with, prompting them to clarify what Christians really thought and did in their worship. The offshoots are called *tritheism* and *monarchianism*. Tritheism contends that there were three eternally existent and separate gods who created, redeemed and sustained the universe. Tritheism is like a cosmic democracy (or better yet, a Roman triumvirate of three equal leaders) comprising three gods. Monarchianism, on the other hand, held that one God, the Father, was superior to two other lesser gods: Jesus and the Spirit. Like a cosmic kingdom, monarchianism has one absolute King and a couple of helpful but subordinate princes.

Obviously, neither tritheism nor monarchianism is true to Jewish monotheism. While they provided a possible explanation of how Jesus of Nazareth and the Holy Spirit were related to the Creator, they removed Christianity as a religion of one true God. There were other problems as well.

A variation of monarchianism, for example, taught that the single, all-powerful God—the Father—loaned some divine power to the man Jesus and adopted him. (The adoption is thought to have occurred at Jesus' baptism [Mt 3:17; Mk 1:11; Lk 3:22].) Thus Jesus was more than an ordinary man but less than God. Thus there was one God and a lesser semidivine helper (or two). This view, of course, raised questions about the lesser status of Jesus and about the nature of the Holy Spirit, who was viewed not as a person but as an energy, effect or byproduct of the real God (just as a music CD is the byproduct of an artist's creative energy; the effect, product or attribute is not the same as the originating person). This position came to be known as *adoptionism.* Jesus was adopted by God, and the resulting power in Jesus was the Holy Spirit. Hence, one God and two lesser agents: Jesus and the Holy Spirit. However, why would Christians worship the lesser gods? Wouldn't this be idolatry?

In tritheism, monarchianism and adoptionism Christians are not true monotheists but are idolaters because they do not worship the one true God alone: "Hear, O Israel: the LORD our God, the LORD is one" (Deut 6:4). Christians in these cases were breaking the first commandment: "You shall have no other gods before me" (Ex 20:3).

Another possible way of viewing the Father, Son and Holy Spirit is that each is a different manifestation of the same one God. So, when God created the world, God was revealed as Father; then during the time of Jesus, God came as the Son; and since Jesus' ascension, God is known as the Holy Spirit. This theory is called modalism. *Modalism* is the idea that one Being (God) shows up in different periods in different roles, depending on the purpose of God. For some Christians this seemed a perfect solution, but there is a big problem. During the time of Jesus, God seems to be less than omnipotent or all-powerful, being on a vacation of sorts, slumming around with humans. And who exactly was Jesus praying to on the cross? Who was Jesus addressing when he said, "Father, forgive them" (Lk 23:34) if he is the only God? And why did Jesus pray, "My God, my God, why have you forsaken me" (Mt 27:46)? Was it merely a charade for our benefit, or was it truly a dialogue between God the Father and God the Son? Modalism created more problems than answers.

Early Christians needed to clarify what they were doing and thinking. They worshiped Jesus of Nazareth, the Holy Spirit *and* the (monotheistic) God of the Jewish faith; they baptized each other in the name the Father, Son and Holy Spirit; and they believed that Jesus Christ was their Savior and Lord. These practices are doxological—that is, what Christians do is really where theology starts. An early Christian slogan articulates the relation between Christian practice and theology: the "law of praying is the law of belief" *(lex orandi, lex credandi)*, or the "expression of our worship of God, Jesus and the Holy Spirit forms our thoughts about God, Jesus and the Holy Spirit." No church should take this lightly; what we believe is a reflection of what we do and vice versa. This is why the doctrine of the Trinity was hammered out among Christians, because they did not want to be misunderstood as affirming tritheism, monarchianism, adoptionism or modalism—all of which were found in the Mediterranean and Eastern religions. Christians were monotheists in continuity with the Jewish revelation of God as one God who alone created, saved and sustained God's people.

THE CONSTANCY OF THE LOVE OF GOD

Why did the early Christians make their belief in God so complicated? If they worshiped one God who was identified as three separate yet interrelated divine persons—Father, Son and Holy Spirit—why not simply carry on without probing this mystery with theological arguments? The answer lies in the fact that the religions of surrounding cultures had many similarities that threatened the integrity of Christian worship. If Christians could not work out the differences, it was possible many would be persuaded (or deceived) to worship other gods. The marketplace was full of religious options, and Christians had to be able to help other Christians distinguish between true and false faith and worship. Some religions posed a grave danger for Christians because they sounded *very* Christian. These were the Greco-Roman family of religions that scholars would later call *Gnosticism*. There were different varieties of Gnosticism, and *Marcionism* was a specifically Christian off-shoot.

"Gnosticism" is derived from the Greek word for knowledge, *gnōsis*.

18

It usually refers to religious societies that claimed to have secret knowledge about the nature of God, the created world and salvation. Gnostic groups thrived for hundreds of years (and variations continue to this day). A Gnostic is someone who claims to have new knowledge or revelation of God. Although there were many different groups, Gnostics shared the following characteristics: (1) the created world was a mistake or the unintended byproduct of a cosmic argument or action that occurred in an eternal and spiritually pure heaven; (2) the material or created world, our world, is either imperfect, polluted or a mere stage in a greater cosmological drama; (3) human souls, or some spiritual spark or memory, fell from the spiritual realm and became encrusted with matter (the human body); and (4) it is humans' duty to learn their true (spiritual) identity through secret knowledge *(gnōsis)*.

For Gnostics the material world, which includes our bodies, is inferior to a deeper spiritual existence, and in some cases the created world is the kingdom of a trickster, an evil and malicious lesser divine being. Each Gnostic group claimed to possess secret teachings (and actions) on how its members could escape the material world—the tyranny of the flesh and the demonic creator—in order to return their spiritual selves (souls) to their former spiritual existence and the true God.

For "Christian" Gnostics, secret knowledge came from Jesus of Nazareth, who was not the true God but served as God's messenger. Sometimes Jesus is merely a human who has been given special insight, and sometimes he is an archangel or some other high-ranking divine creature. But Jesus is not, for the Gnostics, the one true God.

In response to Gnosticism, Christians began to think seriously about the doctrine of creation. That the world was created by some cosmic being or beings was a given in the ancient Near East. What distinguishes the Christian view, picking up from Jewish teaching, is that the material world is both good and created from nothing *(ex nihilo)*. God created a flawless world and declared it "very good" (Gen 1:31), and further, human sin doesn't offset God's purposes for creation. The universe was created from nothing, that is, by God's will alone, and not from the debris of some cosmic accident.

Keeping this overview of Gnosticism in mind, we can begin to understand the threat it posed to Christianity. First, if Jesus was not God, how could Christians be certain they were actually redeemed? Could Jesus himself be wrong about God and salvation? Maybe deeper spiritual truths lay hidden in the mystery of God. Could humans be certain of *anything*, including salvation? Imagine the anxiety of not being sure, particularly when Christianity was an illegal and persecuted religion. Because Christians didn't participate in the civic worship of local gods or the emperor, they were thought of as bad citizens. Why suffer for Jesus if he was not the Savior?

Second, Christians not only worshiped Jesus as God but also believed Jesus was really human—a material creature. This made them double idolaters: (1) they did not worship the one true God, and (2) they worshiped a *creature*—a human, which neither the Jews nor the Gnostics found acceptable.

Let's recap. Christians were offensive to many because they refused to worship the public gods, making them civic pariahs; they offended monotheists because they apparently worshiped more than one God; and finally, they offended Gnostics and others because they worshiped an embodied God.

> The Word became flesh and made his dwelling among us. We have seen his glory, the glory of the One and Only, who came from the Father, full of grace and truth. (Jn 1:14)

> And if Christ has not been raised, our preaching is useless and so is your faith. More than that, we are then found to be false witnesses about God, for we have testified about God that he raised Christ from the dead. (1 Cor 15:14-15)

If the Gnostics were correct, there was no salvation in Christianity, only misinformation.

In response, Christians insisted on several things, all of which were occasioned by their worship. First, they insisted that there must be no difference between the Creator God, the Redeemer God and the present Spirit. In short, God *now* in the church as the Spirit and *then* in Jesus Christ is the same as God *before* creation. For early Christian theologians and leaders this meant that the entire *economy of salvation*—the entire history of God's interaction with creation and humanity—includes (1) God, as known by the Jews, (2) Jesus Christ and (3) the Holy Spirit. All of this is part of God's plan for humanity, part of the singular will of one God, who is Creator, Redeemer and Sustainer. Christians rightly worshiped God the Father, God the Son and God the Holy Spirit.

In response to Gnostic teaching that the god of creation is different from the true God, Christians looked to their worship life and apostolic teaching to articulate what would become the doctrine of the Trinity. The doctrine worked to explain the complex experience of Christian worship and salvation: God as Creator, Redeemer and Sanctifier. Christians claim that it has always been, is and will be the purpose of the triune God to create partners to share in God's life and glory, to redeem them, and to be in fellowship with and make holy (sanctify) humans and the created world because of the *constant* character of love within the triune God. God is totally and without ambiguity revealed as Father, Son and Holy Spirit. Christianity's God is the same God as Judaism but is different from the gods of the Gnostics and others religions.

Christians can be assured that Jesus is God, that the Spirit in their midst is God, and that Jesus and the Spirit are in fact the same as the Creator God. Each person of the Trinity possesses the same Godness (substance or essential nature) and purpose (will or intention toward humanity). In the plan or economy of salvation, to know one member of the Trinity is to see all the others, because the Trinity shares the substance, purpose and love of the one true God.

Early Christians used the word *perichoresis* to describe this sameness of substance and will. Perichoresis is the way Christians tried to articulate their understanding that the God they experienced and knew in Jesus and the Spirit was the same God of and before creation. Perichoresis was a working backward of sorts, a way to understand that the different divine persons experienced by Christians—Father, Son and Holy Spirit—are in fact one God. By beginning with their experience of the Spirit, of the person of Christ and Judaism's monotheism, Christians considered after the fact that each member of the Trinity must be the same God. Working backward they concluded that to know one member, by definition, was to know all members of the Trinity, lest monotheism turn into tritheism. One God, one will in all, and to know one member was to know God.

Perichoresis means that the members of the Trinity are so interrelated that we cannot easily distinguish between them *even* in terms of their respective roles. In a very real and unique sense the interior relationships of the Trinity are part of God's existence. Another way of understanding perichoresis is that the divine persons mutually indwell one another, such that the indwelling is actually part of the description of each divine person. The Son, for example, is only the Son as far as the Father and Spirit indwell the Son, and so forth. There is no *mine*, only *ours* in the Trinity. All the members of the Trinity are involved in the same grand eternal project, which is to love humanity and creation. No one member of the Trinity can be parsed out of that grand project without reference to the other members. Jesus Christ is the love of the Father and sustained by the love of the Spirit. The Spirit is sent to Christians as the love between the Father and Son in agreement to create and redeem humanity and creation. The Father is given glory by the work of the Son as the expression of love and is now known by the Spirit, and so forth. Each one leads to the others. To speak or experience one is to speak and experience the others. It is *appropriate* to speak of the members in terms of the dominant task each has, but each's task is not exclusive to that single member of the Trinity. All are equally God and at once God, and one God alone. All are worshiped.

THE CONSTANCY OF THE REVELATION
OF GOD'S IDENTITY

The first Christians were Jewish, and the early Christian leaders had important conversations on the relationship of Christianity to Judaism, particularly whether a person needed to be Jewish in order to become a Christian. The New Testament is largely an account of this question. By the end of the first century, Christians had come to a conclusion that (1) to become a Christian a person did not have to first convert to Judaism, (2) Christians shared the same history and paternity with the Jewish people, and (3) Jesus Christ, the pivot point of the Jewish experience of God, had opened for non-Jews what had previously belonged exclusively to Judaism. Christianity and Judaism are expressions of the same God.

Every Sunday morning the early Christians gathered to recount the history of God with humanity, and particularly Judaism, in order to publicly confess that the God of the Old Testament is the God of Jesus, whom they worshiped and glorified as Lord. The Christians affirmed that the God of the Hebrew Scriptures is *their* God, that they can trust God's promises in *those words* to them as revealed by the Creator, Savior and Sanctifier. Further, they affirmed that Jesus Christ and the Holy Spirit are one with *that* God.

Nonetheless, as more non-Jewish people converted to Christianity a new wrinkle developed in the Jewish-Christian relationship. Marcion (c. A.D. 110-160), heavily influenced by Gnostic thought, taught that Hebrew Scripture—the Old Testament—was a mixture of truth and error in its presentation of God. He argued that it contradicted the new stories of the Christian writers and Gospels. Marcion felt that the Jewish God—Yahweh—was actually a lesser god whose temperament and actions were in opposition to the true God revealed in Jesus of Nazareth. Jesus' God was a God of love; Moses' God was a god of wrath.

Therefore Marcion and his followers edited the Jewish sacred texts; anything that did not fit with the God of love was removed. They also questioned the history of God with Israel and the nature of Jesus' relationship to Judaism. In the long run, Jesus was not Jewish!

Consider the implications of what Marcion and his followers did. First, they challenged the usefulness or truthfulness of the Hebrew Scripture as the revelation of God's will and purposes, including its description of creation, God's interaction with humans and salvation itself. Second, they challenged the relationship that Jesus had with the Hebrew God. Pandora's Box was opened. If Marcion's teachings were true, Christians could not be certain that the God proclaimed each Sunday morning was the true God. And the relation of Jesus to the Hebrew God was in doubt.

The development of the doctrine of the Trinity was neither a metaphysical game nor intentionally obscure. It is instead the product of the earliest Christians making sure that their thought matched their Sunday practice—worship of God by reading sacred texts and celebrating the sacraments of baptism and the Lord's Supper (Eucharist). In response to quasi-Christian approximations, such as Marcionism, the doctrine of the Trinity, which was implied in the Scripture, was slowly clarified.

WHAT IS THE DOCTRINE OF THE TRINITY?

Part of the problem with the doctrine of the Trinity is the limitations of human experience and language as we try to explain the greatest mystery of faith. *Mystery*, for theologians, does not signify something that is impossible to know or articulate, but rather something that the human mind *by itself* cannot come to an independent knowledge of. Before we can begin thinking about this mystery, God has to tell us about it. This is revelation. Then, after receiving God's revelation, Christians can think deeply about the matter.

Understanding a mystery of faith is similar to knowing another person. We can know nothing of another person if we don't know that he or she exists. Once the person's existence is revealed to us, we can discover certain things about him or her by doing a background check or asking others who know the person. But a deep understanding of that person can only come by having personal interaction with him or her—that is, the person reveals his or her own self. When Christian theologians speak about the mystery of faith, they are saying that we know God only as God self-reveals.

Through the ages, Christians have thought that despite the imprecision of human language, it is nonetheless important and even appropriate for us to try to articulate those mysteries of faith. Sometimes this is called *appropriation,* or the process by which Christians use language (primarily analogies) to describe a fundamental truth. The use of appropriation in the Trinity demonstrates this point. When discussing one particular person of the Trinity, a certain quality or work is sometimes given special prominence in order to underscore a theological point, but it is important to remember that this does not mean that that quality is exclusive to that member of the Trinity. For example, it is appropriate to speak of the "eternity of the Father, the truth of the Son and the love of the Spirit." In each case a quality, such as Jesus' revelation of God's character, is underscored, but this does not mean that the Father and the Spirit do not reveal truth. When humans speak about God, and especially the Trinity, they must use ideas and analogies that help but do not fully express the deep reality of God.

The classic definition of the Trinity was most firmly articulated in the great Christian council in Nicaea (A.D. 325), the basis for the Nicene Creed. The early church determined that the Trinity is one God sharing one substance (Greek *homoousia,* Latin *consubstantia*) of Godness in which three masks (Greek *hypostases,* Latin *personas*) are manifest and, due to the nature of all being of one substance (Godness or *homoousian*) itself, are by definition mutually inherent (perichoretic) in the other members of the Godhead. It is important to realize that masks for the ancients are meant to indicate "stock" roles in a play rather than remind the audience of actors playing a role. Masks then reveal easily identified "jobs" or "types." It was natural for theologians to consider that the members of the Trinity were identified by their "jobs" but revealed a common will and substance. This means that the persons of the Godhead are distinct but not divisible *(distincti non divisi, discreti non separati)*. We cannot speak of one person without needing to also describe the others. We cannot separate, rank or order the Godhead as if it comprises three independent beings or gods.

The doctrine describes what the Trinity is by saying what it is not: it is not three gods (not divisible) or three different modes of God (not distinct).

The Trinity is hard to imagine, so theologians have offered several analogies. Some of the more common and useful ones are

1. *Spring, stream and fountain.* A spring, stream and fountain all flow from one another and share the same substance: water. Where the water is can be distinguished (a spring, a stream and a fountain), but it is not separated. This explains *homoousia*—the continual property of water always being water whether in the spring, stream or fountain, and we cannot have a spring, stream or fountain—which are the *hypostases*—unless there is water.

2. *Chain.* There are many links in a chain. One or two links do not make a chain. When a link is connected to another link in the chain, it is connected to all the others. This explains perichoresis.

3. *Rainbow.* In a rainbow all the colors *(hypostases)* are evident, yet all are the same light *(homoousia)*.

These are examples of appropriation: using human references to speak of God. When we use analogies, we need to be aware that we can never separate Father, Son and Holy Spirit. They are not like the divisions of a big company: God Inc. They don't have separate interests, accounts and personnel. Instead, each "office" is totally and completely God Inc., and each represents all the interests, accounts and personnel fully without any reduction of those interests, accounts and personnel. To visit one office is to have experienced all the offices of God.

THE DEMISE OF THE TRINITY

Despite the absolute centrality of the Trinity in Christian life and thought, the doctrine has had long periods of marginalization in Christian history. There are usually two reasons for this. The first has to do with how Christians relate to their environments. Early Christians differentiated their beliefs and practices from those of other religions, and then went about living as faithfully as possible. But around A.D. 1750, Western Christians felt threatened by new ways of thinking that challenged what they believed. In response Christian theologians felt compelled to articulate what they had in common with other faiths and belief systems, and they tried to explain Christianity not by what Christians *practice* but rather by what made sense to those outside the Christian community. The earliest Christians answered the outsider with "We are not like." But in the modern period, perhaps because the intellectual world was outwardly Christian, theologians responded to ideas outside Christianity with "We are like."

At that time, the doctrine of the Trinity was not seen as the natural outgrowth of Christian worship in response to God, but as a political structure that reinforced the power of certain people. The great ecumenical councils (Nicaea and Constantinople) of the early church were not viewed as *theological* councils but instruments that served the interests of an emperor and bishops. Theologians have a special word for this view: *Dogmengeschichte* (history of dogma). The dominant assumption is that doctrine does not to help Christians think about worship or common life, but is always constructed for human gain.

Thus the great mystery of the faith—the Trinity—lost its theological punch and was relegated to the back shelves of Christian thinking. This why Friedrich Schleiermacher (1786-1834), one of the greatest of Christian theologians of the nineteenth century, tucked his discussion of the Trinity into the conclusion of his theological text!

The second reason for the demise of the Trinity is related to the original problem that the early Christians faced. The Trinity was articulated because the Creator God is the same God Christians worship in Jesus, their Lord and Savior, the same God whose presence was manifest in the reading of Scripture and the celebration of the sacraments. However, during the modern era some Christians changed their view of the nature of Jesus Christ. Somewhat like the early Gnostics, modern theologians began to think of Jesus as a human with either a heightened awareness of God or some internal divine principle that could be shared with all people. Jesus, therefore, is not the Son of God in the trinitarian sense but rather is someone who has a highly developed sense of God. Instead of being the divine Redeemer, Jesus was the founder of the community stimulated by his example and teachings to do good and love others. Jesus is the first and greatest self-help guru. There is no Trinity because Jesus is *not* God.

THE REEMERGENCE OF THE DOCTRINE
OF THE TRINITY

During the twentieth century some leading theologians began to question whether nineteenth-century developments could be called Christianity at all. The most important was Swiss theologian Karl Barth (1886-1968). By understanding Barth we can understand the importance of the Trinity to the Christian faith.

The doctrine of the Trinity reemerged in Christian theology largely for the same reasons it developed in the first Christian communities. The doctrine's significance was recognized in the twentieth century when theologians carefully examined Christians' worship and practice, as opposed to what some theologians thought. In other words they found that Christian practice was trinitarian; Christian life is modeled on trinitarian relationships. God created humans for fellowship, redeemed them for fellowship and sustained them in that fellowship. This God was the God of the Christian community. The church lived in fellowship with that God and therefore had to witness to that God.

The twentieth-century history of Europe was not pretty. It underwent two grievous wars, several attempts of genocide and other evils. European Christians could no longer think of themselves as being part of a great and progressive culture. The myth of a highly civilized Christian Europe was an illusion that had persisted for over 250 years. But by the middle of the twentieth century many theologians felt there must be a better path for the Christian community. These theologians, often referred to as crisis theologians, sought a new way of doing Christian theology. The collapse of Christendom created a crisis in theology.

Between 1914 and 1945, Karl Barth had witnessed two devastating wars, a global economic crash and the rise of a maniacal political power that sought the destruction of the Jewish people. Further, the national churches of Northern Europe and many of his theology professors joined the prevailing agenda. The Nazi swastika hung beside the cross in every German church. Alongside with praise to God, one would praise Hitler! Boxcars of Jewish people were shipped off to extermination camps. "Christian" Europe was ugly.

Karl Barth knew something was wrong with European theology, and he began to probe the right way to think as Christians. Theology, for Barth, should be done by Christians for Christians, to help them live more faithfully. Barth found answers in the doctrine of the Trinity.

Barth believed that European theology had failed to differentiate human culture and the Christian revelation of God. The problem for European Christianity, he thought, was that Jesus Christ was not recognized as the divine Son of God, and the church was not under the command of God the Holy Spirit. Instead, much of European theology was a form of monarchianism or adoptionism. Jesus of Nazareth was not God but merely modeled faith in God. The Holy Spirit was some aspect of human spirituality writ large, which Jesus modeled and demonstrated.

Barth turned to the classical doctrine of the Trinity as *the* Christian description of God. He believed that the Trinity accurately reflects (1) the character of God's inner life, (2) God's interaction with and in creation, and (3) God's definitive revelation in Christ and through the church as it witnesses to Christ.

Barth's summary is that creation is the external basis of God's covenant of grace with man and that this covenant is the internal basis of creation. More simply, the God manifested in creation, in Christ and in the church is the same God who exists before creation. Further, Christians can trust that God's promise (his covenant of grace) to be their God and Savior is an exact reflection of who God is. This God, further, has been and is revealed as God the Father, Son and Holy Spirit. Unlike Gnostic theology, there is no doubt as to whether Scripture reveals God as Father, Son and Spirit. Because of their perichoretic relationship each member of the Trinity is an accurate reflection of the other members. This means that we can be *certain* that the God we know and experience as for us *(pro nobis)* is the same as God really is in God's inner life *(in se)*.

For Barth, it is imperative that the doctrine of the Trinity as Father, Son and Holy Spirit is the only proper Christian description of God. This means that when we see Jesus Christ, we see God: "No one has seen the Father except the one who is from God; only he has seen the Father" (Jn 6:46). The European church, in Barth's opinion, had forgotten this basic truth and had forgotten to be obedient to its theological or witnessing task. The Western church, including Barth's own Reformed tradition, was in apostasy because it worshiped itself, its culture or anything but the Lord.

The doctrine of the Trinity, according to Barth, entails an even larger complex of theological realities related to God's character and love. Because of Christ and now through the Spirit in the witness of the church, creation is being caught up into its true purpose in the divine life of God. Material beings are meant to be with God. Creation was lovingly provided by God, but the cultures within it are under the God's judgment. The church is where the reality of the triune God is revealed, and when the church worships and witnesses, the surrounding culture encounters God. The Trinity is so important that Christian theology must start with this doctrine.

The doctrine of the Trinity for Barth is "three moments" of revelation's "repetition"—three notes of the same musical symphony and message of God's love: (1) God is Lord; (2) God is the one who encounters us and unites us to God and to each other; and (3) God's revelation

30

will transform us when we encounter the divine loving Other. God as Father is the Revealer; as Christ, God is the act of revelation; and as Holy Spirit, God is revealedness (or how we truly know ourselves and live with other humans and in creation). What we do on Sunday morning when we encounter God through Word and sacrament (regardless of our theology) is a crucial act of obedience to the promise of divine presence.

Barth reversed the question of the previous centuries, How are humans able to relate to God? in favor of a new question, How does God speak to humans? and its corollary, What is our response to this speech?

Understanding God as triune is the foundation for human reception to the revelation and therefore love of God. More particularly, because God through the Son has annexed (or more specifically assumed) humanity in the Trinity, the impossibility of hearing God, due to human sinfulness, is overcome by God's action toward us. The trinitarian God is sovereign and Lord, and *that* God comes to us and thereby guarantees our hearing the divine Being, because that God chooses to reveal God in the work of Christ and in the Spirit, whom Christians worship and encounter in the church. We are obedient, fulfilling God's purposes, because God redeems and sustains us. God intends this destiny for all peoples, and it is the privilege of the church to witness to this great reality.

Agreeing with the earliest Christian communities, this means that revelation—Christian confidence that God was in Christ and in their midst as Spirit in the church—is based on and guaranteed by the work of the triune God seen in the incarnation and the history of salvation. Along with many others, Barth has shifted modern theology from a preoccupation with human grounds for revelation (how can we be certain that we know God) to a theology of the Trinity that is implicit in the confessional lives and practices of the church.

The Trinity then is the first great link in our theological chain. The other doctrines follow because in the Trinity we are assured that we find God in Christ, and therefore the redeemed community (church) is really, fully and clearly of God. Subsequently, we also know that

- God is present when Christians celebrate the sacraments and hear the Word of God, and in their prayers and worship.

- God is the Lord, and commands and allows us, because God loves us, to participate in the economy of salvation as witnesses without the worry of how to do it. In other words, as we are faithful to God's claim of lordship, free to love God in that lordship, we are, by definition, faithful stewards and witnesses. God is the origin and source of our mission because God is Father, Son and Holy Spirit. Further, that kind of God is deeply interested in being in and with the church, because that kind of God is present in the Trinity.

The doctrine of the Trinity gives Christians confidence that they *know* God, because God is that God (which is God's nature in any event) who is Father, Jesus Christ and Spirit in the church and world. That God is Lord and reveals God's self to the church and world. Karl Barth will speak of God's self-election as this moment, a way of speaking of the fact that God is interested—so interested that God was incarnated and crucified—in being close to humanity and creation and giving God's self to that world (Jn 3:16). In theory, God could have been disinterested, distant or completely separate from humanity and the world, but instead because God demonstrates in the Trinity God's true nature, God is near as well as Lord. The Trinity is Christian confidence that they know God and this God is present and Lord.

DISCUSSION QUESTIONS

1. Why should Christians think deeply on the doctrine of the Trinity?

2. In your opinion, why is it important that Christians trust that the Creator is the same as God as the Redeemer?

3. If the proper name of God is "Father, Son and Holy Spirit," then how much leeway is there for innovation in naming God, such as "Creator, Redeemer and Sustainer"?

4. Many twentieth-century Christian theologians believe that the interrelationships of the Trinity model how humans should relate to each other. Do you think this is useful? Why or why not? Could it obscure the Trinity?

BIBLIOGRAPHY

Introductory
Augustine. *On the Trinity*. Church father.
Lash, Nicholas. *Believing Three Ways in One God*. Notre Dame, Ind.: University of Notre Dame Press, 1992. Roman Catholic.
McGrath, Alister. *Theology: The Basics*. Oxford: Blackwell, 2004. Anglican evangelical.
————. *Understanding Doctrine: What It Is and Why It Works*. Grand Rapids: Zondervan, 1990. Anglican evangelical.
Hall, Christopher A., and Roger E. Olson. *The Trinity*. Grand Rapids: Eerdmans, 2002. Evangelical.

Intermediate (assumes some undergraduate work)
Fortman, Edmund. *The Triune God*. Grand Rapids: Baker, 1982. Roman Catholic.
Jenson, Robert. *The Triune Identity: God According to the Gospel*. Philadelphia: Fortress, 1982. Lutheran.
Letham, Robert. *The Holy Trinity: In Scripture, Theology, History and Worship*. Philipsburg, N.J.: P & R, 2005. Evangelical.
Moltmann, Jürgen. *The Trinity and the Kingdom: The Doctrine of God*. New York: Harper & Row, 1981. Lutheran.
Weinandy, Thomas. *The Father's Spirit of Sonship: Reconceiving the Trinity*. Edinburgh: T & T Clark, 1995. Roman Catholic.

Advanced (assumes advanced undergraduate to graduate level)
Gunton, Colin. *The Promise of Trinitarian Theology*. Edinburgh: T & T Clark, 1991. United Reformed.
Jüngel, Eberhard. *The Doctrine of the Trinity: God's Being Is in Becoming*.

Edinburgh: T & T Clark, 2004. Reformed.

Kasper, Walter. *The God of Jesus Christ*. New York: Crossroad, 1989. Roman Catholic.

Rahner, Karl. *The Trinity*. London: Burns and Oates, 1970. Roman Catholic.

Zizioulas, John. *Being as Communion: Studies in Personhood and the Church*. White Plains, N.Y.: Longman, 1985. Orthodox.

2

THE DOCTRINE OF SIN

*"For all have sinned and fall short of the glory of God,
and are justified freely by his grace through the redemption
that came by Christ Jesus."*

ROMANS 3:23-24

WHY IS THE DOCTRINE OF SIN IMPORTANT? The answer is quite simple and is related to the fact that Jesus of Nazareth, called the Christ, is our Redeemer. Christians believe that Jesus Christ has redeemed, purchased or released us from *something* (and someone): sin. This Christian doctrine derives from our thinking on Jesus Christ. Paradoxically, the doctrine of sin seems to be the most clear of all truths in the Christian faith. After all, it is the only Christian truth that is readily apparent and universally recognized.

People are not always good. Thus it is easy to think of sin as something we *do*, for example, moral failure. This is how sin is popularly understood (or misunderstood). Our inability to be good may be a symptom of sin, but sin is actually a much more serious disease—a life without worship, without recognition of God, without the hope of a real humanity, which includes our actions. This is what sin is. Sin is living as if God is not who Jesus Christ revealed God to be. To talk of sin, we need to talk about Jesus Christ.

SIN ISN'T ABOUT DOING WRONG THINGS

Dietrich Bonhoeffer (1906-1945), the great theologian and Christian martyr, once commented that God only knows humanity as sinner. What he meant is that God in Christ has redeemed humanity, so *humanity as sinful* is already accepted by God. For Bonhoeffer sinful humanity—us as loved and redeemed by God in Christ—is whom God knows and not some abstract or future perfect person that none of us resemble. The one *truthful* statement about sin is that God loves the sinner. Sin, for Bonhoeffer, remains a problem for humans, but God in Christ has judged it as "no-thing." God is not surprised by sin; in fact, the Christian message is that God has a remedy for sin. We cannot think about sin without recognizing that God has already dealt with sin. To talk about sin is to talk about God. All talk about God, that is, all Christian theology, has two starting points: (1) God's perspective (revelation) and (2) humanity's experience of God.

Starting from God's perspective means working from the revelation of God in Christ to determine how Christians should think about the world and humans. Some basic questions we ask are (1) what did the Son of God come to earth and die for? (2) and What does Jesus' resurrection and ascension mean for human life now? Christians have answered that Jesus died in order that humans might be free from the three great enemies of God—the devil, death and sin—and therefore live in God's purposes for humanity. These purposes are to (1) worship the true God, (2) live eternally in God's presence, and (3) live with God and each other as true humans:

> "Love the Lord your God with all your heart and with all your soul and with all your mind." This is the first and greatest commandment. And the second is like it: "Love your neighbour as yourself." All the Law and the Prophets hang on these two commandments. (Mt 22:37-40)

However, if we look at sin from our perspective (or experience) as sinners, then we come to a different conclusion, which is fraught with concern and anxiety. Here we share the concern of the young Martin

Neurotic
Oedipus

36

Luther (1483-1546), who was preoccupied with his many failings. Luther lived in terror of God's judgment. Instead of worshiping God, Luther spent most of his young life as a monk trying to run from God or doing things to appease God's wrath. Eventually, Luther rejected this perspective when he discovered justification by faith.

Viewing sin from the human perspective has dominated much of what has passed for Christian theology from the medieval period to today. The emphasis is on being good enough, and not the generosity and good will of God. Sin becomes a checklist of moral pluses and minuses, which is weighed out before a cosmic tax collector. But aren't we beyond that today? I don't think so. Many contemporary Christians start at the wrong place. We continue to have a medieval image of sin. To illustrate this, we will look at the ideas of German philosopher Immanuel Kant (1724-1804), a chief architect of the Enlightenment.

Kant lived at a time in which there was an increased confidence in human progress and education. Kant felt that the Christian doctrine of sin, and the doctrine of original sin in particular, were especially grotesque. The doctrine of original sin was that humans are radically and universally sinful. This was popularly understood to mean that even before doing *anything*, humans are conceived in sin and made sinful during the sexual act itself. Before one sin is committed, each human is already guilty.

Kant believed that the idea that human beings are utterly doomed before they are capable of acting created a condition of moral laxity. Kant reasoned that when people are told they never were and never will be good, we should not expect them to try to be good. Further, if they are also told that when they do wrong they can be forgiven through prayer or some act of repentance, then there is no incentive to do anything good. It is easier to ask forgiveness than to do the right thing in the first place. History certainly backed up what Kant observed: people did wrong things all the time because forgiveness was easy. The piety of many Christians was mere lip service to their faith; many were hypocrites.

We must understand that Kant was a serious man who knew his Bible. He knew that sin *was* a problem, and that good Christians follow the teaching of Jesus about love of God and neighbor. What then was the problem with Kant?

Kant had the wrong starting point. He assumed that what is really important for Christians is to follow the content of Jesus' teachings. The cross of Christ is only important to Kant as an example of how a good person might endure bad things to demonstrate sincerity of belief and the depth of ethics. Christ is a great figure of ethical purity, a Gandhi for his time. In Kant's account, then, to be a sinner is to reject the ethical teachings of Jesus' higher truths. Kant had a problem with Jesus as the Christ; he missed the significance of why Christians pray to, worship and praise Jesus. Christ died *for* sin, not simply as an example of what a good person can stand for in a sinful world.

THE CHRISTIAN DESCRIPTION OF SIN

The doctrine of sin starts by pondering what Jesus did and who Jesus is, and not necessarily what he said. This sequence is important. For Christians, it is possible to live the kind of life that Jesus prescribed only because of who Jesus *is* and what Jesus *did*. Jesus' identity and his mission are tied together. Simply put, because of what Jesus *did*, he reveals who he *is*, and this frees humanity to live in the purposes of God. The Christian response to this work of salvation is to worship God, and part of right worship is to live rightly. What then is Jesus' work of salvation?

First, we must understand that through the cross, the resurrection and the ascension, Jesus broke the hold that the three enemies of God had on humanity. The enemies of God—sin, death and the devil—are parasites, living off a host (humanity), creating sickness and disease that eventually kill. They have no independent existence. In fact, from the eternal perspective they have no real existence because from eternity the triune God has judged them to be false, defeated and condemned. Under the control of sin, death and the devil, humans live exactly as conceived by Kant—as if they were their own master, controlling their own destiny. This creates the impression that sin, death and the devil are very powerful. But from the Easter perspective they are absurd, even laughable. They, like sin, are "no-thing."

THE DEFEAT OF THE GREAT ENEMIES OF GOD

Regarding the work of Swedish theologian Gustav Aulén's work, Jaroslav Pelikan says:

> At the root of any picture of the Atonement is a cluster of ideas about God, man and Christ. He who says A about God, B about sin, and C about the person of Jesus Christ would seem obliged to go on to say D about the redemptive work of Jesus Christ.

In 1931 Gustav Aulén (1879-1977) wrote a book that explored how Christians have interpreted the death and resurrection of Jesus Christ. The book, *Christus Victor*, was written to counter a dominant understanding of Jesus' work on the cross. While some question the historical accuracy of Aulén's work, his argument is nonetheless helpful. Aulén argues that Christian belief about the cross has been consistent throughout much of church history. According to Aulén, the three major interpretations of what happened on the cross are not unrelated but are facets of the same diamond.

Aulén, along with his contemporaries, believed that Christian understanding of the cross was largely influenced by culture. All humans are conditioned by history and culture, and certainly this is true of Christians. Consequently, it was generally thought that Christian doctrine changed as history moved on. Let's examine the argument in detail.

The initial Christians were superstitious, believing in the supernatural world of demons and angels. They, as a result, understood the cross and resurrection in terms of Jesus' defeat of the forces of evil. God tricked the devil into thinking the cross was the end of the story when it was the beginning of God's work. Using Jesus as bait, God trapped the devil.

Later Christians, more influenced by Greek philosophy, approached the cross from a different perspective. For them, the dominant enemy was death and decay. Jesus' victory on the cross was seen in terms of the defeat of death. What is common in both these views is that the devil and death are *cosmological* or epic in scope. They are beyond human influence; their struggle is with God, not humans.

Many early Christians viewed the cross as a sort of spectator sport. They watched from afar and benefited only indirectly from God's war on death and the devil. True, Christians no longer belonged to false kings (the devil and death), but the shift in kingdoms was an indirect consequence of God's own purposes to eradicate two usurpers. There was little personal application in this change. God's love of humanity was secondary to God's hatred of sin.

The genius of Aulén, picking up the Reformers' later stress on personal salvation, which some thought of as distinct from the cosmic vision of the early church, was to rediscover that while salvation was cosmological it was also an "inner confidence" that the Christian belonged to a new King or new kingdom. It was this placement of the self—you and me—into a cosmic drama that Christians, according to Aulén, were invited to consider. God's love of humanity was primary in God's hatred of sin, death and the devil. Sin was an unfortunate accident of birth, reversed by Christ, who enabled the sinner Christian to be sprung from a spiritual but real prison. In more simple terms, we are sinners, but not only sinners. Aulén takes the two ideas thought to be separated and showed how they were one. But before Aulén was able to argue his point, he needed to deal with another dominating idea of the cross found in the work of the Latin theologian Anselm. Anselm's ideas, at first glance, make sin an even greater problem, rather than casting it as a reality overcome by God's work in Christ.

Anselm of Canterbury's *Cur Deus Homo (Why the God-Man)* is an important book in Christian theology, and how one reads it is imperative in understanding sin. Anselm lived between A.D. 1033 and 1101. His idea of the cross suited a culture in which the Christian church was a central and powerful reality that stood tangibly and visibly in the life of Christendom. What was needed here was an equally legal understanding of the cross—an understanding that fit the monolithic presence of an absolute church and its leadership—and thus the cross became not the defeat of the devil or death but a legal transaction between God and humanity. The cross became a law court, where sin was punished by God, paid for by the substitution of an infinite innocent in Christ for a guilty humanity whose offense to an infinitely worthy God meant only an infinitely innocent person could satisfy God's wrath. Anselm's theology of satisfaction seems to offer some measure of release from sin, as he argues that Christ satisfied God's wrath in a unique manner undertaken by God alone. But unlike the first two understandings, which are cosmic and allow some measure of personal application, there is a cold legal logic to this external reduction of the cross. In the defeat of the devil and death, Christians could live differently now because they lived under a new King, but in some readings of Anselm it was felt that Christians *really* didn't live under a new King, or at least they didn't until death. In the meanwhile, it was imperative that Christians kept a close watch on their deeds and prove worthy of that great formal legal transaction done on the cross and which they might find eventually applied to them.

What happened was that Christians became preoccupied with their worthiness or even evidence of that distant legal transaction by God. Imagine being set free from a prison, but the legal paperwork is in a far country. One sits and waits for the paperwork to arrive, tries to act as if one is actually free, and perhaps even expects treatment worthy of an innocent person by one's jailors. How the newly freed prisoner behaved—pretending to be free or avoiding further trouble that might again result in imprisonment—was really more important than the actual papers because that formal legal freedom was a long way off. Until that legal reality comes true, the prisoner is best to behave and to act as if free even while still in prison. The façade is more important than the promise. So there was a problem with each of the ways in which Christians had thought about the cross and therefore about sin.

In the cases of the earliest Christians and their cosmological understanding of God's battle with two usurping would-be kings, the devil and death, Christians were almost a byproduct of a more important war in heaven. Sin, the reign of the devil and death, was defeated but there was little personal application in this far off reality. In the case of Anselm, the technical language and cold logic also meant sin was a preoccupation—or the lack of sin was evidence of being worthy of the legal judgments of God. In both cases, sin is a preoccupation, and Christians, rather than seeing themselves living in graced love, tend to become accountants of moral piety. The final piece of the puzzle of sin occurs with the Enlightenment and the thought of philosophers such as Kant, as indicated above. What happened is simple. When sin is merely an understanding of one's moral standing, it becomes very easy to think that one can be educated out of sin. Sin in the modern mind is not an enemy of God, something God has dealt with on the cross, but instead something to be overcome. Just as for the audience that read Anselm to consider sin as a list of dos and don'ts, so sin becomes a miseducation of our higher selves. Aulén thought this to be incorrect. Why?

Aulén starts by answering that all three enemies are to be understood by the cross, not by historical situation or even as a way to explain the cross, because all three are related to each other. Jesus Christ as the revelation of God on the cross demands in his resurrection that Christians think of the enemies of God in a certain way. Namely, Aulén argues that each of those enemies of God is to be understood as defeated. This entirely reversed the theological opinion of the day, which began with what each of the enemies of God meant for humans and then worked back to God as a result. In particular, Aulén argues that the logic of the cross defies human systematization, not in terms of understanding its meaning for salvation, but in terms of understanding *what* really happened in the miracle of the God-man. It was, he argues, exactly Christian unbelief or disbelief in defining sin, death and the devil that created the problem of modern theology with its attention to making at least two of the enemies of God (the devil and death) into mythological conceptions and therefore reducing the third (sin) to a category unfamiliar to Christian theology.

As Christians rejected the idea of the devil and understood death in terms of human potential, so the argument against sin as a sin against God in favor of an understanding of sin as sin against one's humanness became prevalent. The cross of Christ became a symbol of human love or another description of a human being willing to endure in order to win something great. It was not, according to Aulén, a description of the work of God but rather a description of the work of human example. Aulén argues that with the rise of skepticism toward two of the enemies defeated by the cross, the third enemy—sin—was also changed. But what did the cross mean?

CHRIST THE VICTOR

Aulén reversed the theological opinion of his day by arguing that throughout church history Christians described the cross of Christ as a victory over *all* God's enemies. There was no evolution or development in thought. Though theologians sometimes highlighted certain aspects of the cross, they recognized that all three of God's enemies were overcome by the victory of Christ. There is a measure of perichoresis (interpenetration) in speaking on the enemies of God.

At all times in Christian theological articulation, the enemies of God are understood as usurpers, tyrants and parasites in God's good creation. These enemies are *cosmological* in that they seemingly reign over all of creation—the game seems rigged for their benefit and gain—but they are also *personal* in that each human is under the thrall of the enemies. However, and crucially, the enemies live on borrowed time and in borrowed space; their rule is not absolute and complete. The truth is the reality of God as revealed in Christ and through the work of the cross. From the foundation of the world, that work of God at Gethsemane is a continuous act of grace that streams backward and forward in human history.

God's enemies are revealed to be shadows and nothingness before the real King. Christ is not only the victor for individual Christians but also over all of creation. The cross of Christ, then, is the true description of the enemies of God because it alone reveals the enemies' true status before God—powerless, self-destructive and defeated. Aulén argues this is *the* longstanding theme of the church when it comes to the cross and the enemies of God.

But how are the enemies related? The fall of humanity, which was actually the rise of human arrogance, created a space or vacuum into which a usurper entered to set up a false kingdom. The devil, by this account, *seemingly* was given rights over humanity and the created world. Human self-deception about their own independence from God allowed the prince of lies to dissemble about the nature of the cosmos, portraying himself—the devil—as the end of all things. Death became the bludgeon wielded by God's enemy to force humanity and creation to submit. Humans and creation seemed to be in the spiral of death. Thus all roads lead to despair.

The relationship between death, the devil and sin is clear: sin created an empty space and the devil became a squatter; sin created the fear of death because death signaled the judgment of God. But what if that judgment was not what we believed it to be? What if God forgave sin, and therefore death was not the end of the human story? Wouldn't this remove the devil's bludgeon? Wouldn't this expose the devil as a thief, liar and usurper without any real power? The cross tells *this* story, and it begins with sin.

SIN THE ENEMY OF GOD

Perhaps the best description of sin is living as if God did not exist. All manifestations of sin, whether personal or social, stem from the false assertion that God is not God. This can mean many things: (1) rejecting God's revelation about God and humanity, and worshiping ourselves or created things; (2) denying in others the essential dignity of being created in the image of God and treating them as objects to be

44

abused; (3) living as if I am my own god, living to satisfy my own means and rejecting any limitation of my desires, hopes or wants. According to Paul, Augustine of Hippo, Martin Luther and John Calvin, these are some of the more common Christian definitions of sin: *idolatry, self-centeredness (in se curvatus)* and *misordered desires* (cupidity). What unifies these is sin as selfishness—living in a false freedom wherein God is deemed irrelevant and humans become abusers of self and others in an effort to feed a hunger that cannot be satisfied. The cross of Christ, however, speaks another truth: humans are created to be in fellowship with God. *This* destiny defines human life and purpose because it is what the triune God intended, won and sustains.

In Christ and his victory on the cross, to use the language of Karl Barth, we learn the deep truth that "humanity is for God" and "God is for humanity." Any other assertion is a falsehood and sin. Living as if we are not for God and God living as if God were not for humanity is shown to be a false way of being. Sin opens humans to the devil and death. But the cross, God's universal and radical declaration of human worth, affirms that no one is exempt from God's love and will, and exposes the miserly existence God's enemy's offer. *Christus Victor* is the only cry of Christians!

SIN IN MODERN UNDERSTANDING

The Western world is reluctant to part with one of its most precious and hard-won ideas over the last few centuries—that there is no limitation on human freedom or potential, including God. Moderns understand humans as autonomous or independent selves who, given enough hard work and planning, are free to choose, out of a myriad of possibilities, their own destiny. A person simply makes a plan and works it out. Moderns have no time for sin because it denies the fact that humans answer to God for their existence and for their choices. It also denies the fact that freedom, from the Christian perspective, is circumscribed by a loving God. Moderns believe humans float above all context, situation and even self-limitation; human desires and self-will can produce something out of nothing. Christians reply that only God makes something out of nothing; humans are God's beloved creatures.

Theorists refer to humans as "Man the Maker" *(homo faber)* because human ingenuity has created wonderful technological and cultural solutions and advances. And this is also thought to be true in terms of human potential. Sin, as articulated by the philosopher William James (1842-1910), is a morbid remnant of a past era, whose only purpose was to keep people under the thumb of the church and state. It belongs to the trash bin of human ideas. The concept of sin limits human potential because it suggests that we are bad. After all, if a young boy is told he is worthless, won't he come to believe he is worthless? Thus moderns rejected or reinterpreted sin.

If the term *sin* was going to be kept, it had to be reinterpreted. Thus the doctrine of sin came to be understood two ways: (1) personal failure to be a true person (or true to the need to be happy), and (2) corporate failure of a society to be true people (or to create a climate in which people could prosper). In the first case, sin is an individual's failure to be actualized or "healthy-minded." In the second, it is the failure to build economic or political systems that help people fulfill their potential and freedom. These views of sin are characterized by two philosophies: existentialism and Marxism.

Prior to the rise of existential philosophy, which arose in the late nineteenth and early twentieth centuries, human freedom was strongly tied to personal morality. For example, Immanuel Kant argued that the Christian view of sin was useless for morality because it created either a "sin now and get forgiveness later" mentality or moral indifference because humans were destined to be immoral. What was the incentive for being good? Kant argued that there was none. The Christian doctrine of sin broke an inherent moral standard or golden rule. That there is a moral standard, or even what it might be exactly, is now admittedly imprecise on reflection. But Kant and his followers believed that through clear rational thinking the "good" could be determined and also obeyed. God was merely the source of the rational law found in the human mind. To be fully human was to be moral, and to be moral was to be free. Kant ruled European thought until the moral atrocities of the nineteenth and twentieth centuries, which challenged the sobriety and rationality of Kant and his progeny.

Existentialists believed that the beginning of the Kantian project was flawed because deep within was the lurking notion of God. Existentialists argued that from the Kantian perspective, God had planted the notion of the moral good within humans. This meant that failure to be good or moral might result in future punishment by God. The existentialists argued that the Kantian understanding of sin and morality implicitly depended on a punishing, wrathful divine being. This was no better than the primitive beliefs about God and the terror of sin. This understanding of God and punishment only created neurotics and immature people. Both Kantian thought and the old Christian ideas Kant tried to replace undermined human responsibility and relied on a fairy tale of hope. Humans needed courage to be something else, something that allowed them to face their true nature.

The existentialist movement had a slogan: "Existence is our essence." What they meant was that this present life or existence is the only life we have. As such, *we* are in charge of our own personal happiness. We will create our own destiny only when we soberly face the absurdity of life itself. For the existentialists it is absurd to think that there is some sort of correspondence between our behavior and what happens to us. Bad people prosper and good people suffer. The existentialists taught that the only way to live is to seize every opportunity to make ourselves authentic. Life may be hard, but we control those things that we can and find our pleasure and meaning in that. Authentic living is not about God, eternal life or even moral choices (although we might be moral), but about making choices and learning to live with consequences. Leave the "bad" behind, focus on the "good" and work to the best. Sin then is denying the freedom to choose, denying one's own inner voice, and denying another person's freedom to choose his or her own identity. Sin is both personal (self-effacing unfreedom) and corporate (enabling others to persist in the state of self-effacing unfreedom).

Christian existentialism interprets Jesus Christ's teachings and actions as helping individuals see their higher selves and live in faith in the moment of choice. Faith is not faith in God or even God's presence, but rather faith in one's ability to choose to be a whole person in the midst of a confusing world. This is the understanding of sin of many popular TV self-help gurus. A "sinful" person is one who does not believe in him- or herself. We must be true to ourself.

The other dominant understanding of sin in the modern period takes its cue from the philosophy of Karl Marx (1818-1883). Like the existentialist movement, Marxism rejected Kant's view on the nature of human freedom, God and the afterlife. Marx similarly thought this world is the only world. But he was not concerned with the inner or psychological life of humans but chose instead to understand human life in terms of real-world objects such as money, food and other goods. For Marx, human behavior is shaped by their response to material objects. Individual identities and societies are formed in response to the environment, material needs and the scarcity or overabundance of products. Whether on purpose or by accident, wealthy and powerful people figured this out and, as a result, disseminated ideas to reinforce their privileged position on the top of the material pyramid.

Their very best idea was religion and its promise that in the next life there would be recompense for the woes of economic and political injustice. Poor Christians could sing of and pray for a better world to come, and in the meantime they would remain content in their sorrowful situation. Marx, however, believed that when people understood the world's material foundation, they would revolt and create a new way of living that addressed the economic, political and religious imbalance. The result: a new utopia of cooperation. "Sin," a word Marxists would not use, is to continue in the old way of thinking, which included religious dogma. Those who persist in sin are afraid of forging a new material, political and religious world based on the principle of equality or communal life.

Marxism is attractive to many Christian theologians. After all, didn't Jesus teach a similar vision of society in the kingdom of God? Aren't Christians supposed to refuse privilege to persons based on their status in society, and don't they call each other "brother" and "sister"? Even Karl Marx admitted that the Bible portrayed a nearly pure, if eventually disabled, form of socialism or common good by the first Christians. As a result, many Christian theologians, particularly those who lived with the marginalized poor or socially disadvantaged, saw in the Marxist critique a way to understand sin. Sin for them is the dominant society's values of privilege, power and wealth.

This critique has several positives. It tries to address the impact of sinful institutions on the lives of everyday people. It argues that poverty drives poor people to steal, that miseducation can lead to abuse, that wealthy, talented and highly educated are often given legal or state power to abuse others under the auspices of civil order. The use of material forms (products, capital, goods and services) in order to subjugate other people is sinful. Sin is everywhere and nowhere. We are born into sin, yet it is something we learn and contribute to unless we alter our paths. Sin is "external" to us (we are born into an environment of sinful humanity), but we also internalize it when we agree to participate in the propagation of sinful structures of power and authority. (This last point parts company with Christian theology.)

The greatest problem with the Marxist and the existentialist understandings of sin is that they reduce the personal and triune God to a principle of justice. God is like a map placed over culture (or the self) to see where various things are. Or imagine God as a sort of large-scale CAT scan machine we use to peer into the human body and see what kind of medical procedure is required to cure the ailment. But the link between diagnosis and actually undergoing the medical treatment is broken. Knowledge is *mere* knowledge. By definition the Marxist understanding of sin only understands the complexities of the material world as factors in deciding how people choose to live. Even if people are aware that they live in, participate in and even create an unjust world, there is no compelling reason to live any differently.

In the Christian Marxist reading, if an individual sees in Jesus an example of a new communal way of life in which all things are shared and in concord, the real question is, so what? Why should one person give up privileges in order to elevate another if there is no God or afterlife? The mere idea of community isn't enough. Certainly the poor are motivated to change things; they stand to gain in the new world order. But once they are in a position of power, will they be any better than those who previously held power? Why should the rich and powerful change? Just because it would be nice for people to act according to a greater calling of justice and peace? Perhaps remembering being personally oppressed aids such a disposition, but as history has borne out, the reality is much different. There is no reason to change, to go from sinner to saint, apart from personal fancy. Further, evil people don't frequently change, and even those who overthrow an oppressor are often found to be as corrupt as those they replaced. Except for the example of a few great people, human nature does not change. (And even in the case of those who do, don't look too closely lest they be revealed as having clay feet.)

The problem with Marx's view of sin is that God doesn't exist. Therefore sin is what we make it out to be. And the Christian Marxist understanding, while noble, is just one out of many possible human choices. And here is the ultimate irony: scholars have pointed out that Marxism works only against the backdrop of Christian Europe because Marx assumes so much theology in his critique. The *idea* of God lurks in the background, for humanity is only *obliged* to live in peace and justice before God. While Christian Marxists got that part right, the question remains: how do people live in peace and justice before God without the cross of Christ?

THE CROSS OF CHRIST AND SIN

The cross of Christ reveals that humanity is God's and God is for humanity. It reveals that the God who created is the God who redeems and sustains creation and humankind. This story affects every human regardless of location, worth, education and so forth. It is the revelation that the mystery of human rebellion (sin)—living as if God isn't God, or being out of step with the nature of God as revealed in Christ—isn't the end of the human story. Nor is it the end of the history of humanity with God. Rather, God anticipated and willed another story, which is the continual history of God with humanity, despite and in the midst of sin. The cross reveals that God overcomes human folly by offering to humankind its true destiny once more, exchanging with humanity what is God's own life in order that humanity might have what the Son of God knows and is. The cross reveals that the enemies of God are usurpers, utterly defeated and under the feet of Christ.

Death and the devil are not the end of humanity, but life with God is. The cross reveals that in taking human flesh, as willed from eternity past and now revealed in the fullness of time, God knows human suffering and what evil can do: it put the Son of God on a shameful cross. Therefore no marginalized person, no person who knows the pain of life's absurdity or human evil, needs to walk alone, without a God who knows that pain, evil and sin. If that kind of pain, evil or sin were the end of the story, then all would be lost and there would be no hope. The cross offers another vision: human hope grounded in God's purposed love and covenant to walk with humankind.

The cross of Christ tells us we have real hope in the transformation of ourselves and the world. Nothing can impede God's will and purposes. The cross places our neighbor before us, not as an idea, platitude or principle but as one equally created and loved by our Lord. The weakness of the Marxist position—why change?—is overcome by the claim that each person is dearly purchased and released to fulfill his or her true life, which is fellowship with God and pursuing justice for others. Our vocation as redeemed people is to be stewards of that gift. Our call as redeemed people is to live in obedience to that goal. As redeemed people we are to live in the freedom of that reality. On the cross of Christ we see ourselves as free. And therefore we see our neighbor's good as our obligation and duty in order to live in our original freedom.

I have coined a new term that describes this: *Christomorphic metanoia*. *Metanoia* is the Greek word for "repentance" or "changing one's mind." *Christomorphic* means "being forged into the image of Christ." The cross is not merely the idea of this change; it makes change possible because it reverses the curse of sin and its opening us to the enemies of God. The cross is where repentance becomes possible and is the place from which the Spirit of God is unleashed for Christians to live as Christians. From the cross, *from God's perspective*, sin is seen not so much as a fate or a condition to be pitied but as a tyrant with a weak hold over humanity. The cross reveals that the freedom offered by culture is a false friend, that living in sin is impoverishment or no life at all; instead only in God are we finally free. To love God is to worship, which is not a burden. The cross redresses the problem of original sin. Because of the cross we don't worry about how to find a gracious God or our worth before God. Obedience is driven by being loved and sanctified. The love of God exhibited on the cross therefore formulates a true ethic based on worship. It means God doesn't leave us alone, even as sinners. It means seeing sin through Easter eyes.

DISCUSSION QUESTIONS

1. In your own words explain what sin is.

2. Given a theology of sin, how should Christians deal with sinful persons?

3. Explain how Jesus Christ has defeated the enemies of God.

   What does that mean for you?

4. What do existential and Marxist theologies of sin do well?

   Where do they need to be corrected in order to help Christians think about how they live?

BIBLIOGRAPHY

Introductory

Ramm, Bernard. *Offense to Reason: A Theology of Sin*. San Francisco: Harper & Row, 1985. Evangelical Protestant.

Plantinga, Cornelius, Jr. *Not the Way It's Supposed to Be: A Breviary of Sin*. Grand Rapids: Eerdmans, 1995. Christian Reformed.

Intermediate

Bonhoeffer, Dietrich. *Creation and Fall*. Philadelphia: Fortress, 1996. Lutheran.

Brunner, Emil. *Man in Revolt*. London: Lutterworth, 1959. Reformed.

Niebuhr, Reinhold. *The Nature and Destiny of Man*. New York: Charles Scribner's, 1941. Protestant.

Schoonenberg, Piet. *Man and Sin: A Theological View*. Notre Dame, Ind.: University of Notre Dame Press, 1965. Roman Catholic.

Advanced

Alison, James. *The Joy of Being Wrong: Original Sin Through Easter Eyes*. New York: Crossroad, 1998. Roman Catholic.

Farley, Edward. *Good and Evil*. Philadelphia: Fortress, 1991. Protestant.

Krötke, Wolfe. *Sin and Nothingness in the Theology of Karl Barth*. Princeton, N.J.: Princeton University Press, 2005. Protestant.

Pannenberg, Wolfhart. *Anthropology in Theological Perspective*. Edinburgh: T & T Clark, 1985. Lutheran.

3

THE DOCTRINE
OF THE INCARNATION

"In the beginning was the Word, and the Word was with God, and the Word was God. He was with God in the beginning. Through him all things were made; without him nothing was made that has been made. In him was life, and that life was the light of men. The light shines in the darkness, but the darkness has not understood it."

JOHN 1:1-5

WHY IS THE DOCTRINE OF THE INCARNATION, the coming of God in human flesh in the person of Jesus of Nazareth, important? The incarnation is the fulcrum between God's intentions as revealed in the Trinity and the human problem as revealed in the doctrine of sin. The incarnation is God's love letter to sinful humans and the ground of God's promise to be humanity's God, to be present in the church and to restore all of creation. Without the incarnation, God remains abstract and distant, humanity is left to itself, and creation is disposable staging to be ignored or mistreated. Creation and humanity are not important apart from the incarnation. But the incarnation tells us something about God, about humanity and about the material world. Humanity is designed for God, who is its partner and lover. And creation—matter—is endorsed by the incarnation.

Of course, the incarnation raises many technical and difficult issues, particularly the relation between Jesus' humanity and divinity. These questions, however important, first need to be couched in some more essential terms, which we will examine in this chapter. When Jesus asked "Who do you say I am?" (Mt 16:13-16), Peter responded with what others were saying. The technical aspects of the incarnation, such as the relation of Jesus Christ's two natures, are what "they," or rather we, think about Jesus. This is important, but it is secondary to what God says about Jesus. But first, let's see what the world tells us about Jesus.

JESUS IN THE WORLD

Sensational works such as Dan Brown's *The Da Vinci Code* may seem new or cutting edge, but their ideas about Jesus are actually very old. Ever since Christians began to talk about the resurrected Jesus, people have had commonsense explanations that make him ordinary. But Jesus of Nazareth is anything but ordinary! He is the incarnation of God—literally, the invisible God in human flesh. Jesus proclaimed *who* God really is, *what* God really desires for humanity and creation, and *how* humanity is to live. But the Dan Browns of history make Jesus merely human, and not God incarnate. We will look at three examples.

Jesus the wise. Jesus undoubtedly had special insights into what the world would be like if we all treated each other with respect regardless of race, creed, color or social status. If everyone has the same Father, then we all are brothers and sisters, and we should work for a better world. Perhaps he even had an enhanced consciousness of God as our Father. But though Jesus may have been extraordinary in some ways, he was *merely* human. This view of Jesus as a wise sage and teacher of an ethic of tolerance and mutuality is characteristic of liberal Protestantism. One of Karl Barth's teachers, Albrecht Ritschl (1822-1889), summed up this view in a slogan: Christians believe in the Fatherhood of God, the brotherhood of humanity and the future ethical kingdom of God. The church is where the ideas of fraternity, equality and liberty to do right are cultivated. Of course, all this, while heroic, is really rather ordinary.

Jesus for the liberal Protestant is a wise *man*, a first-century Obi-Wan Kenobi whose teaching is understood in terms of fraternity, equality and justice. And the biblical texts, though still respected as a source of information about Jesus, are reread or edited to reinforce the ordinariness of Jesus. The Bible is a historical document about Jesus that speaks in terms of its own unique time. Thus the Bible's historical sections and the wisdom teachings needed to be separated from the supernatural elements to make it palatable to the modern reader. This struck many well-educated Westerners as perfectly sensible and entirely appropriate. Liberal Protestantism promised a way to leave behind centuries of superstition and discord over religion, and to foster a new golden age of culture.

Perhaps the most famous example of editing the Bible is Thomas Jefferson's *The Life and Morals of Jesus of Nazareth* published in 1829. Jefferson was a deist, believing in a rational or explainable God. Deists are ancestors of liberal Protestants, but we should be careful to distinguish the two groups. For Jefferson, the Creator God (if God exists) is like a grand clockmaker who makes, winds and starts the clock, and then leaves the clock to keep its own time. God created the universe and is now observing as it runs by its own laws. Following the philosophy of Immanuel Kant, Jefferson wanted people to be responsible for their behavior, to desire to be good people. He felt that the worst possible thing a person could be told is that he or she is forgiven. This, Jefferson thought (as did Kant), created two problems. First, it creates a passive morality; people do not have to work hard to build moral character, resting in God's election and forgiveness. Second, it also creates a more insidious passivity in civic duty. Religion, according to a Jefferson, leads people to think exclusively about the future (heaven) and not about the present. Therefore religious people are not active or diligent in their civic responsibilities. The problems of the present world, including ignorance and poverty, are off the radar of the pious. Religious piety is selfish, being directed toward meriting heaven. To Jefferson, traditional religion was ignorant superstition. Superstition led to confusion, confusion to disorder, and disorder to the impossibility of peace and progressive culture.

Like the liberal Protestants that would come later, Jefferson thought the simple ethic of Jesus was lost in the superstitious universe of the first centuries, which included miracles, healings, exorcisms and, worst of all, the incarnation. Humans need the pristine morality of Jesus the wise man, not the metaphysical rhetoric of a God-man. Jesus' message, according to deists and liberal Protestants, was simple: follow the golden rule—"Do to others as you would have them do to you" (Lk 6:31).

Jesus the pious artist. While Jesus was merely human, he was also extraordinary in some regards. But extraordinary does not mean supernatural. Jesus was extraordinary in terms of his *faith* or confidence in God. His spirituality is an example for humans to follow; it is what real faith looks like. Jesus cultivated his spirituality or inner self in such a way that he most closely resembled a person living *as if* he were God's intention for humanity. He alone, of all humans, most clearly lived the spiritual life and therefore possessed the highest possible spiritual destiny or maturity. Thus Jesus may, as in the theology of Friedrich Schleiermacher (1768-1834), be thought of *as if* he were the Son of God in that he most closely resembles a person living in the fullness of God's purposes in creation. Jesus best portrays a spiritually alive person; he is a superavatar of God. Further, as we observe Jesus' feeling for the holy, we can cultivate our own personal piety. This is the key to aesthetical theology, which does not stress the rational mind but human sense or feeling. The artistic, or that which appeals to the heart, opens us to God.

In this perspective the biblical portrait of Jesus needs to be rescued from the Greek philosophy that influenced the early church. Jesus' Jewish heritage needs to be restored. The parables of Jesus, which are poetic or artistic, are truer to the real Jesus than the teachings of Paul. Paul was a good metaphysician but a terrible poet. Likewise, the Synoptic Gospels are favored over the Gospel of John, because of the charged imagery in it. The supernatural Jesus and the claims of the first Christians (such as Paul) need to be reinterpreted to reveal the piety or God consciousness that Jesus exhibited, taught and spread to his followers.

These visions of Jesus as sage and artist suffer in many ways. One of the most problematic issues is the inherent elitism. One needs to be well-educated, cultured and have a life of leisure to ponder the aesthetics and wisdom of Jesus. One of the most often repeated criticisms of the two movements is that in both cases "it takes a Jesus to invent Jesus." That is, these visions of Jesus require a genius to interpret his meaning for the rest of us. The "ordinary" Jesus is almost impossible to discover except by an extraordinary interpreter. This introduces the final school of a Dan Brown, one whose most influential proponent was a German biblical scholar named Rudolf Bultmann (1884-1976).

Jesus the existentialist. Rudolf Bultmann thought that the Bible was a document accessible to all people, regardless of education or culture. He argued that the true message of the Bible is to create faith in God's future for each human person—or, in more common terms, that God loves and has a plan for each person in death and certainly in life. Everyone from the youngest to the oldest, least to most educated and across cultures can grasp that essential truth in the Bible. However, there is a problem with the Bible. Jesus taught as a first-century Jewish man. And early Christians also used the only culture they knew: first-century Greek culture. Both Jewish and Greek culture were couched in the myths—demons, angels, god-kings—and philosophy of their time, which needed to be demythologized (i.e., removing the period's relics for a new day). In the process of reading the Bible, Bultmann felt, the human spirit encounters faith—God's basic message of possibility and hope—and this message is able to cross cultural boundaries. But, and this is important, it also means that the reader or hearer needs to learn what is and is not essential to that message. The essential truths behind outmoded myths need to be explained in terms understandable to the modern mind. Bultmann and his followers disagree on how active God or the Spirit might be in this process, but almost all agree that the human spirit is at least a coagent in interpreting the Bible and its relevance.

Bultmann's demythologization seemingly recognizes faith as a theological category instead of merely being rationally or aesthetically insightful. It also allows room for the faith of a poor farm worker as well as that of a university professor, who obviously will respond differently to the same biblical passage. But it still makes Christianity a largely human phenomenon; the supernatural or supranatural aspects of the Bible (and Jesus) are discounted (demythologized) in order to find the true Jesus. Thus, like Schleiermacher and Jefferson, Bultmann finds an extraordinary Jesus, but not a supernatural Christ. Jesus is not the unique God-man but rather the best example of what is naturally human. Jesus is different from us in degree, but not in kind. Does this really matter?

Let's think of Dan Brown's vision of Jesus. He is a good man, perhaps even an important man in terms of his vision and message. Perhaps we could go further with Schleiermacher and argue that he is so close to God in his piety that we will never see a better approximation of a human before God. Perhaps we could even go further with Bultmann and say that Jesus was so close to God that his message is able to create in us a "Jesus faith" in God's love and purposes for us, regardless of who or what we are. But we must also agree with Sir Leigh Teabing, one of Brown's characters, and think that somewhere something went wrong in the transmission of Jesus' message. Somewhere along the trail of history, Jesus' message got lost or was co-opted by unscrupulous people. We need to peel away the barnacles of history to get a fresh look at Jesus. Then we may feel awe in the presence or message of Jesus, and if particularly moved we might bend our knees before him in respect. But we should not worship him as *the* incarnation of God. He remains a thumbnail sketch, an approximation of God, our best guess or even our hope.

But that is the problem. Is human hope enough? Should we stop all this nonsense about Jesus and instead follow his simple message of humane love for each other? That is the message of the world's Dan Browns. Jesus should never be thought of as the incarnation of God.

THE UNAMBIGUOUS COMING OF GOD

Michael Ramsey (1904-1988), British theologian and archbishop of Canterbury, best summed the incarnation's importance when he argued that it means *not only* that Jesus is God but more importantly that God *is* Christlike. Let's ponder what this means.

Clearly one of the problems for many people when it comes to understanding God is the problem of "projection," articulated by the philosopher Ludwig Feuerbach (1804-1872) and the psychoanalyst Sigmund Freud (1856-1936). For both men, God is merely humanity-plus or a projection of what, were we able, we would like to be. God is all-powerful, all-knowing, all-present and unchangeable because, as humans, we are exactly the opposite. We are frail, limited, localized and changeable beings. Thus Feuerbach and Freud, joining many others in history and in the present day, argued that God, or the idea of God, is merely humanity's wishes and hopes magnified. What this has classically meant for theology, then, is that the idea of God is usually charged with being superhumanity, and Superman (the comic hero) is the closest image to what people would like to be—always good and superpowered. The ancients, however, didn't quite have the imagination to think of a "Superman" (always good) and instead settled for a flawed set of gods such as Zeus or half-gods such as Hercules. Zeus and Hercules, in the Greek stories, are powerful but so very human too, complete with envy, anger and sexual lust. Better philosophers such as Plato (428-347 B.C.), however, thought that a flawed or impassioned superbeing (having human foibles such as anger, lust and jealously) was antithetical to the idea of a perfect reality or Being, and as such for him "God" had to be unchangeable, distant and without "passion."

One can easily see how the ancient world (when it came to thinking about "God") presented a problem for the first Christians. For some Jewish Christians whose Jewish God could be understood as jealous, angry and certainly involved in the everyday life of Israel, the "Zeus" model could be attractive. God was to be continually appeased, kept happy, and a Christian earned God's favor. For a Greek Christian, it is easy to think of God as Plato did. God is far off, without passion and certainly unable to truly interact with humans or humanity's daily issues. Both are rather, in the end, unappealing visions of God. One is a temperamental child, and the other is a disinterested parent. But instead think on what Archbishop Ramsey said about the importance of the incarnation—it is not so much that Christ is God (even though this is true) but rather that God is Christlike. This is a radically different way of understanding God—God is not humanity-plus, but rather something new is added in the incarnation to understanding God and humanity. A radical description of God and God's way of dealing or interacting with creation and humanity is stressed in the coming of God to flesh. What are these things? Paul explains:

> For the message of the cross is foolishness to those who are perishing, but to us who are being saved it is the power of God. For it is written:
>
> > "I will destroy the wisdom of the wise;
> > the intelligence of the intelligent I will frustrate."
>
> Where is the wise man? Where is the scholar? Where is the philosopher of this age? Has not God made foolish the wisdom of the world? For since in the wisdom of God the world through its wisdom did not know him, God was pleased through the foolishness of what was preached to save those who believe. Jews demand miraculous signs and Greeks look for wisdom, but we preach Christ crucified: a stumbling block to Jews and foolishness to Gentiles, but to those whom God has called, both Jews and Greeks, Christ the power of God and the wisdom of God. For the foolishness of God is wiser than man's wisdom, and the weakness of God is stronger than man's strength. (1 Cor 1:18-25)

Paul tells us that in Christ we see the *unambiguous* coming of God.

And the incarnation, which includes the cross and resurrection, is of such a different quality that neither Plato nor a pious Jew could have declared the nature of God in the same manner. God is Christlike. But what does this mean? It is a description of the *crucified God*, which is the true nature of God, who is near, forgiving and freely chooses to be humanity's partner.

THE CRUCIFIED GOD

Let's imagine being first-century people. First, as common Greco-Romans, we worship the gods daily, having some favorites but making sure that we offend none. We believe the gods have the same kind of interests and desires (including sexual) that we have. Like us, gods can be motivated to act on behalf of favorites, and our worship is an attempt to gain their favor. We offer the gods food and certain actions, and we expect a return on our investment. An individual god is powerful enough to aid us and might even select our group or city as its seat of power. Worship is therefore a part of a civic "defense budget" alongside the payment of soldiers and other city officials. If a calamity happens—a natural disaster or enemy attacks—it is likely because our god (or the gods) was not appeased or perhaps, and more shocking, was defeated by a more powerful god (see, e.g., Josh 3–4). In that case, we change allegiances.

Second, we are Greco-Romans who have read Plato and largely reject the popular understanding of the gods. Such capricious gods are unworthy of worship and as such lead not to piety but rather to neurosis. It is better to avoid all superstition, and teach fraternity and equality alone. In short it is better to be a philosopher.

Finally, let's imagine ourselves Jews. We believe and hope in a God who is near and who works to bring about the prosperity of Israel, which has been chosen by God for a special destiny. Our God is a deliverer who acts in the history of our nation. In the midst of enemies, we wait for God to come to our aid in order to give Israel the Promised Land and peace. And thus Israel will live as a people defined by the rule of God, an island of God in the sea of many gods. Because we have yet to experience this vision, we long for the promised Messiah—a hope of deliverance from foreign masters and their gods.

Now imagine that we hear of Jesus of Nazareth and are fortunate enough to be in Jerusalem during the last week of his life. As a common Greco-Roman we observe he has some power and speaks with authority (see Mt 8:5-13). This sits well with our understanding of what a god might be. As a learned Greco-Roman we might be impressed with the teachings of Jesus, his wisdom, insight and common sense on matters of morality, duty and the hearts of people. Further we might even be impressed by his willingness to suffer and perhaps die for lofty principles. Finally, as a Jewish person, we might be impressed by his miracles as a sign of God's deliverance from Rome, long promised by the prophets (see Lk 4:16-19). We might be leery of the extremity of his claims, which border on blasphemy, but perhaps he could be the Messiah. Of course, not everyone would think the same, but Jesus seems to fit people's expectations of what a god, God or Messiah might be. Then he dies. Not only does he die, but he is crucified—hung on a tree. For the Greco-Romans, this is not only unworthy of a god but more importantly is a *criminal's* fate. For Jews, this is a curse by God (Deut 21:23; Gal 3:13). All three groups would walk from the cross thinking that nothing new about the gods or God has been told.

The scandal of the cross tells us something *new* about the nature of God. Not merely that Christ is God, but rather that God is Christlike.

The Christlike God as the incarnation of God. While in prison awaiting his death Dietrich Bonhoeffer wrote: "God let himself be pushed out of the world unto the cross. He is weak and powerless in the world, and that is precisely the way, the only way, in which he is with us and helps us."[1] Bonhoeffer is telling us that Christ is not only a model of long-suffering pain (the option often understood by medieval Christians), but *as crucified,* Christ reverses the way we think about God as

---

[1]Dietrich Bonhoeffer, *Letters and Papers from Prison,* ed. Eberhard Bethge, trans. Reginald Fuller et al. (New York: Macmillan, 1953), pp. 360-61.

all-powerful, distant and a periodic mechanic who pops into the world to correct misalignments. Instead of a distant or capricious God, we have seen in Christ who God really is—One who is near, who forgives, who repairs human folly and recreates human purpose, who eternally chooses to be that kind of God. God saves. God is Christlike. This Christlike God has several facets for us to consider.

A God who is near. It is quite easy to think of God as all-powerful. This has been the dominant way of understanding God in Christian history. But it entails a huge problem—it makes God appear distant from and disinterested in creation, the nations and individuals. During the late medieval period (A.D. 1000-1500), people thought of God in terms of an absolute king. Just as a medieval king was absolutely powerful and at the apex of a vast hierarchy (and therefore isolated from most people), so too was God. The theological term used to describe this is "the theology of glory" *(theologia gloria).* (Initially the theology of glory referred to God's triumph over all enemies. But it also came to imply God's distance from the affairs of the world.)

People approached God just as a loyal subject approached the absolute king—under strict rules of protocol that ensured the subject is worthy to be in the presence of a great king. Medieval Christians became obsessed with meriting the right to visit or supplicate the powerful King. An individual's life was considered relatively unimportant unless he or she could gain the King's attention. These ideas—God's distance and meriting an audience with God through extraordinary deeds of piety—were problematic during the Reformation. Martin Luther rediscovered the crucified God. Luther's "theology of the cross," the Christlikeness of God, proclaims the nearness of God.

In the theology of the cross *(theologia crucis)* Luther and those who followed him emphasized the scandal of the cross, which is foolishness and a stumbling block (1 Cor 1:23) to our natural disposition to understand God (natural theology). The logic of the Greeks and Jews taught that God would be neither powerless nor die on a cross. More importantly, the theology of the cross reminds us that God is Christlike. God cements God's relationship to humanity and creation through weakness. God did not come to us in all his blazing glory. Through the man Jesus and his death on the cross, the heart of the "hidden God" *(Deus absconditus)* is revealed. In the cross the sovereign King came near to us. God alone is the agent of reconciliation. No human is worthy of it, and no human conceived or anticipated God's work on the cross. It turns everything upside down.

For Luther, when humans look at the cross, nothing about it makes sense. So they have one of two attitudes toward it. Some are disdainful and reject the cross as revelation about God. Others become so bewildered by the mystery of God that they doubt they can merit God's special attention, so they trust God to mercifully come near to them. Luther called this "faith"—trusting in God's promises alone and recognizing that God alone maintains relationships with humans despite their folly and sin. This is who God has always been. Faith, for Luther, is a gift of God (Eph 2:8). On the cross God is revealed to be Christlike, which means God is near in a way that humans would not naturally consider. This encounter initiated by God reveals that God was never far removed from us! The cross is the very heart of God and God's interaction with humanity.

One way the cross demonstrates God's nearness has become a salient picture of God in the twentieth century, which reminded us that despite all our technology and progress, we are still capable of much evil. German theologian Jürgen Moltmann (1926-) is most closely associated with the nearness of God as seen on the cross. Though Moltmann's views of the Trinity and Christology have upset some Christians, the theology I wish to highlight stands easily within Christian orthodoxy. In *The Crucified God* (1972), Moltmann, following Luther, argues that the cross reveals God's true character to a world that has made God in its own image. Writing at a time of great civil unrest and disillusionment with modernity, Moltmann reminded Christians of the apparent weakness of the cross, which pinpoints God's solidarity with the powerless and oppressed. As a position of weakness, the cross tells us that we cannot, must not, put God in a box. For Moltmann, God speaks on God's own terms. More significant for Moltmann, the cross exhibits God's presence with those who suffer, and exposes the roles of those who oppress and inflict suffering on innocents, whether actively or passively.

Moltmann first draws attention to God's solidarity with those who suffer. Because Christ suffered, God knows suffering. Moltmann picks up on a theme in Hebrews which informs us that Jesus is not a high priest who is unable sympathize with human struggles but rather understands them and pleads on our behalf that grace may abound in the time of trials (Heb 4:14-16). Paul and Peter similarly argue that Jesus understands and sustains us in our sufferings, even those we inflict on ourselves by sin (see Phil 2; 1 Pet). Jesus is not just an example of suffering, but rather because God in Christ knows human suffering, we are gifted or graced with God's presence. By knowing suffering, God transforms hopelessness to hopefulness, as the cross demonstrates.

Moltmann realizes that God's solidarity with those who suffer is not the only truth found in the cross. The cross more importantly describes God's victory and a new mode of being in the world. The cross is not the end of Jesus' story. In the resurrection, God affirms Christ's divinity and the absolute defeat of the enemies of God. This has two important implications. First, those who cause others to suffer are enemies of God, working against God's intentions for creation and humanity. Second, God is always near, even when it seems otherwise. The cross is the *promise* of God's presence. And God's promise is always also reality. When God is present, we experience transforming hope (evidenced in the resurrection of Jesus).

The cross—which reveals that God is Christlike—helps us understand that God is not impassible (unfeeling or incapable of suffering pain), or distant from humanity and creation; God is so near to both humanity and creation that our follies are miraculously transformed by God's near presence.

A God who forgives, re-creates and repairs. To paraphrase patristics scholar Maurice Wiles (1923-2005), when we think about the incarnation of God in Christ, the source of salvation must be God, the location of salvation must be humanity. More correctly, the "humanity" Wiles refers to is the God who became human, who stands in the place of all other humans. Theologian Emil Brunner (1889-1966) succinctly spoke of Christ as Mediator. This is another perspective on the truth that God is Christlike.

In *The Mediator* (1934), Brunner wrote that the incarnation is a mediation, a going back and forth or exchange, between God and humanity. God first comes to humanity so that we learn God's Christlike nature. But just as important, the incarnation is also what Karl Barth called "the humanity of God," or how humanity comes to God. That is, the incarnation is how creatures come before the Creator, how the finite comes before the infinite, how the temporal comes before the eternal, how the sinful come before the sinless. Jesus as the incarnation of God mediates—brings humanity—before God. So there's a twofold aspect to the incarnation: (1) God condescends or comes to humanity, and (2) in Jesus, humanity is lifted to God. This is good news! The incarnation reminds us that the triune God is essentially for humanity; God is humanity's partner and lover.

The incomprehensible divine Being is not incompatible with humans. From eternity God has elected, freely chosen, to be in fellowship with humans despite their running from, denial and even mocking of God. Barth often said that God *is* human. He did not merely mean that the God-man Jesus Christ had a fully human nature (which is true) but that because of the incarnation God affirms, stands up for and is involved with humanity. Humanity by nature is to have a spiritual life with, in and under God. This truth is not erased by human action or denied by human fabrication. It is the essential truth of humanity. God and humanity belong together.

"There is one God and one mediator between God and men, the man Christ Jesus" (1 Tim 2:5). At the heart of this rich metaphor is forgiveness. Jesus is our mediator in that he describes God's nature, is an example of how to live as a Spirit-filled (pneumatic) human and teaches about the ethical life in the kingdom of God. But he is also much more. Jesus Christ tells us that humanity is not isolated from God, nor is God from humanity. Because Jesus is the true human, all humanity is likewise God's partner and lover.

Jesus is the Word of God, the self-speaking of God, the embodiment of God's own name. That name is *Immanuel*, "God with us" (Mt 1:23). He is also *Yeshua* (Jesus), "God saves." Together these names reveal that the incarnation (God with us) is God's salvation. And salvation is more commonly known as forgiveness. Our forgiveness means that though we were once far from God, we are now brought near to God, and no human or created force can separate us. Christ is Mediator and Reconciler. Jesus is the witness to and guarantor of God's free grace, but he also is the witness to and guarantor of human gratitude toward God. We praise God for our salvation because Jesus Christ has exchanged what is properly his (sonship) for what is properly ours (sin). God is forever "God for humanity," and because of the incarnation humanity is forever "humanity for God."

The normative human status, regardless of sin and folly, is the beloved of God. When we are asked, Who is the real you? the answer is God's loved one. This is proved in the incarnation, by God in Christ.

Images of salvation. Through the centuries Christians have used several different images for salvation. The Eastern Orthodox tradition and many of the Greek-writing church fathers use the term *deification (theōsis)* in their soteriology or doctrine of salvation. We are saved to be our true selves, Spirit-filled beings in life with God. Deification is the process of growing into true spiritual maturity; it is participating in or enacting that truest reality by being like God *(homoiōsis theōi)*. Deification is *not* leaving human or material life behind in order to become a superspiritual, quasi-divine being. That is, deification is not becoming god. It is, rather, becoming more of what we already have been given (and therefore *are*) in the victory of and exchange with Christ. More simply, deification is becoming our real selves as lived in the glory of God. It is what heaven promises.

Deification is not a work but rather a falling into a way of living that begins with worship and allows God's Spirit to progressively lift the Christian into God's life. This is why the entire Orthodox church's physical space, icons and liturgy are portals to heaven. Church, icons, sacraments and Scripture are foretastes of truest reality, and as heaven bleeds into our worlds in common worship we learn of our truest home. We do not earn this, but it is graciously given to us in our worship.

This Orthodox motif of salvation reminds us that the incarnation of God points to our real citizenship, in spite of our folly and sinfulness.

The magisterial Protestants such as Martin Luther and John Calvin (1509-1564) viewed salvation as forensic justification. This view is prevalent but often misunderstood in contemporary Protestant and evangelical circles. Forensic justification relies heavily on Anselm of Canterbury's influential book *Why the God-man? (Cur Deus Homo)*. Anselm stressed the unique work of God in Jesus and the uniqueness of Jesus. During Anselm's time, many popular devotional movements understood Christian faith in terms of following the example of Jesus in suffering *(imitatio Christi)*, which sometimes translated into extreme models of self-denial and asceticism (e.g., whipping the flesh while on pilgrimages). For Anselm, people were paying more attention to pain, sin and the devil than to God. He felt the world was cruel enough, so he stressed that because God had already dealt with sin, Christians did not have to. While Christians should be sober-minded toward sin, they should not try to repeat the work God had done on the cross through asceticism. Christ died for sinners, therefore we do not need to add anything further to that work.

Just as Luther and Calvin would argue, Anselm emphasized that the incarnation was necessary due to the nature of the human offense before God. Every sin (or transgression) required either satisfaction (making right) or punishment. Further, the payment due is determined by nature of the person offended (and not the offense itself, which is what some Christians thought). In the popular imagination sins were ranked as more or less severe, and different acts of repentance were required, in proportion to the kind, type and frequency of the sin. The "penitentials" were great volumes cataloging all imaginable sins and the required work of repentance for each. In response to this popular piety, Anselm turned to the idea of *satisfaction*. Satisfaction means fulfilling the primary obligation owed to the offended party. Because God is infinite in all things and humans already owe everything to God in terms of existence, any transgression against God, however minute, is an offense of infinite proportion. *All* is already expected. God is perfect, and therefore nothing sinful humans can do to honor God is possible. Anselm argued that the entire system of weighing sin is ridiculous because every offense to God, no matter how trivial, is of infinite consequence.

God is justifiably angered and offended by human sin, which must be punished, but God also loves humanity. Humans must pay, but they cannot because they are finite. Only an infinite being could offer the proportionate act of satisfaction. In order to accomplish both, God must become a human. Jesus Christ, who is human, sinless and divine (and therefore infinite), offers satisfaction to God on behalf of humanity. To answer the question Why did God become human? Anselm responds that only the God-man could provide God and humanity what is needed for the forgiveness of sin. Humans could never satisfy God on their own initiative or capacity. Therefore God intervened.

This appears to be a legal plea bargain between God and Jesus whereby humanity is given a loophole around the problem of sin. Christians have sometimes charged that Anselm, Luther and Calvin's forensic justification is a legalist theology, but this is an overstatement of how each viewed the Christian life (see chapter four). For now, it is important to understand that *forensic* simply means salvation comes from outside human nature and initiative. It is God's action in Christ, God's initiative to repair the irreparable, that Anselm, Luther and Calvin wanted to stress.

Luther and Calvin were uneasy with the prevalent idea in Western Christianity (often called Bielism) that there was some worthy aspect of human nature that might be offered to God. Thus humans could cooperate with God in salvation. Anselm, Luther and Calvin stressed the unique gift of Christ and the free nature of salvation to *all* persons. Forensic justification simply states that in the incarnation and work of Christ what is properly God's becomes humanity's and what is properly humanity's becomes God's. This happens outside of any merit, attribute or quality of humanity. Salvation comes to humans because God is love and chooses to love the sinner. Salvation is possible because of God's character, which is demonstrated unambiguously in Christ.

Many modern theologies shy away from sinfulness and try to find a more positive way to speak of salvation (see chapter two). As with any overstatement of Christian teaching, modern theologies are problematic, but they can also be useful. A common contemporary theology sees salvation in terms of "authenticity"; salvation is finding authentic human existence. While the definition of authenticity and its relation to Christ varies, the intent is that salvation is a deepening of the human self and its experiences. Very often authenticity is thought of in sociopolitical or economic terms. So, authentic life within the salvation of God means working to transform inhumane practices and power relationships (whether personal, social, sexual or economic). Salvation is the radical inversion of those power structures, which is demonstrated in God's salvation history in Israel and Jesus Christ.

Christians who view salvation in terms of authenticity remind us that salvation is never merely private. We are called into the world as an agent of transformation. After all, God entered creation to transform it. In Christ, our relationships are transformed by the renewal and re-creation of God so we can minister to others in proportion to our gifts, temperament and maturity (Rom 12).

Each of these images of salvation reminds us that salvation is God's initiative in overcoming human folly. God's persistence gives us the hope of deification, the reality of justification and the ability to live as authentic people.

A God who persists/elects. The doctrine of election is one of the most difficult Christian teachings. Surprisingly, it was not much of a problem for much of Christian history because it was usually applied only in terms of salvation and the incarnation. For example, Augustine of Hippo (354-430) argued that from before creation God elected (chose/ knew) those who would accept the gift of grace in Christ. But Augustine couched election in terms that stressed the security of salvation and not God's arbitrary choice (see Rom 9; 2 Pet 1). For Augustine, because God alone is the source and guarantor of salvation, then no Christian could foul up God's plans by doing something so terrible that grace was rendered moot. Election, for Augustine and Luther, is a statement of security and not about who is in the club.

Augustine and others certainly have spilled a lot of ink on the relationship between God's foreknowledge and human action, and much of it has been less than helpful. Unfortunately, election, particularly in the theological work of Theodore Beza (1519-1605), a follower of John Calvin, lost its moorings and became a test for salvation. The logical inference also arose that God damned the nonelect. However, there is a *trinitarian* way to understand election. Election, from this point of view, is a description of God's essential character of love, and it sees the incarnation as the summation of God's character.

The Trinity is complete in itself (aseity) and experiences no need. Thus the divine decision (election) from eternity to be humanity's lover is astounding, and it declares God's character of love. The triune God does not need another partner or friend to be completed, to be more divine or to love. In freedom God nonetheless creates and chooses to be *for* creation no matter what. God wants to be humanity's God, and humanity is invited to be with God, destined to be included in God's life and attached to God's own destiny. This is the truest reality, highest truth and greatest mystery.

The humanity of God is declared unambiguously in the incarnation. Here humans fully and finally find the real miracle of God's unalterable, abiding and sustaining love. In Christ, God reveals God's choice to eternally love humanity. Thus Christian confidence of salvation rests on God's nature alone, and not on human will, feeling or hope. This is the best way to think about election. It describes God's character, which is demonstrated in the incarnation. Election is God's persistence to be our Savior. God is in the incarnation. God is Christlike.

This is the gospel: I am totally free, forgiven and saved because of God's coming, God's nearness, and God's forgiveness, reparation and re-creation. These are rooted in God's incarnation in Jesus Christ.

> Philip said, "Lord, show us the Father and that will be enough for us."
>
> Jesus answered: "Don't you know me, Philip, even after I have been among you such a long time? Anyone who has seen me has seen the Father. How can you say, 'Show us the Father'? Don't you believe that I am in the Father, and that the Father is in me? The words I say to you are not just my own. Rather, it is the Father, living in me, who is doing his work." (Jn 14:8-10)

DISCUSSION QUESTIONS

1. In your own words explain the doctrine of the incarnation.

2. Why is it so tempting to think we can earn God's favor? Why is this so problematic for Christians?

3. Identify the image of salvation—deification, justification, authenticity—you are least familiar with. What has it helped you understand about salvation and your relationship with God and others?

4. What does "We preach Christ crucified" (1 Cor 1:23) mean to you?

5. What does the incarnation say about who you are? Who God is?

BIBLIOGRAPHY

Introductory

McGrath, Alister. *Knowing Christ*. New York: Doubleday, 2002. Evangelical Anglican.

Stott, John. *The Cross of Christ*. Downers Grove, Ill.: InterVarsity Press, 1986. Evangelical Anglican.

Witherington, Ben, III. *The Christology of Jesus.* Philadelphia: Fortress, 1990. Methodist.

Wright, N. T. *Who Was Jesus?* Grand Rapids: Eerdmans, 1992. Anglican.

Intermediate

Brunner, Emil. *The Mediator.* London: Lutterworth, 1934. Reformed.

Moltmann, Jürgen. *The Crucified God.* London: SCM, 1974. Reformed.

O'Collins, Gerald. *Christology: A Biblical, Historical and Systematic Study.* New York: Oxford University Press, 1995. Roman Catholic

Placher, William. *Jesus the Savior.* Louisville, Ky.: Westminster John Knox, 2001. Protestant.

Schwarz, Hans. *Christology.* Grand Rapids: Eerdmans, 1998. Evangelical Protestant.

Advanced

Baillie, Donald. *God Was in Christ.* New York: Scribner, 1956. Presbyterian.

Bultmann, Rudolf. *Jesus and the Word.* New York: Scribner, 1958. Lutheran.

McGrath, Alister. *Iustitia Dei.* Cambridge: Cambridge University Press, 1998. Evangelical Anglican.

Macquarrie, John. *Jesus in Modern Thought.* London: SCM, 1990. Anglican.

Meyendorff, John. *Christ in Eastern Christian Thought.* Cleveland: Corpus, 1969. Orthodox.

4

THE DOCTRINE
OF THE HOLY SPIRIT

"But the Counselor, the Holy Spirit, whom the Father will send in
my name, will teach you all things and will remind you of
everything I have said to you."

JOHN 14:26

So God came, overcame sin and gives redemption. However,
aren't Immanuel Kant and Thomas Jefferson correct? Doesn't this mean
we have a cosmic get-out-of-jail-free card?

The doctrine of the Spirit is the theological answer to Kant's and
Jefferson's criticisms. The Spirit is God's presence within the community of Christians. The Holy Spirit enables us to live the way God desires. The Spirit transforms the Christian life, which makes the criticisms of Kant and Jefferson false. Further, the Holy Spirit, the third
person of the Trinity, is the dynamic reality behind Christian ethics
and the church as a community of change. The Spirit, God's gift to
humanity, allows us to live in alignment to God's purposes in the incarnation, bringing all things to their proper end. Christians are privileged to be witnesses or heralds of God's action in the world through
the person and work of the Spirit.

THE SPIRIT EVERYWHERE

The typical Christian today is an African woman in her early twenties who is a neocharismatic. Neocharismatic Christians believe in and experience some manifestations of the presence of the Holy Spirit, often in dramatic fashion, as a barometer of their Christian life. The fastest-growing Christian movement of the last hundred years or so has been the Pentecostal movement. Pentecostalism has its origins in the William Seymour's (1870-1922) 1906 Azusa Street Revival in Los Angeles. However, many scholars find precursors to the Pentecostal movement in the British and American Great Awakenings of the 1700s, in John Wesley's Methodist movement, and in North American frontier holiness movements of the 1800s. Some scholars see Montanism and certain medieval movements as analogs to the contemporary Pentecostal movement. Preoccupation with the Spirit, then, is not a recent phenomenon. Most Christians in the Southern Hemisphere, even Roman Catholics, are more likely to be "Spirit-filled" or charismatic Christians.

Who is the Holy Spirit? Why does the Holy Spirit come?

The Holy Spirit, the third person of the Trinity, is given to Christians and the church (1) as the continuation of Christ's work, (2) as evidence of the love of God in Christ, (3) as the promise of the Christian's future, and (4) as a sign or seal of God's authority. Without the Holy Spirit, there would be no Christians, no church and certainly no hope of living in the promises of God. Thus the Holy Spirit is not an extension of the human spirit or spirituality; the Spirit is uniquely God and has the freedom to work in any manner to continue and enable the work of God in the church. The Spirit's work may be seen in the neocharismatic and Pentecostal revival in the Global South or the experience of the Lutheran, Reformed, Anglican, Orthodox and Roman Catholic traditions.

STARTING AT THE BEGINNING

The Holy Spirit first appears in the Genesis account of creation. There the Spirit or "breath" of God is a doubly operative reality. Not only does God's breath give life to humans (Gen 2:7), indicating that human life is derived and not the same as God's life and Spirit, but also the Spirit is the *fulfillment* of God's creative, loving will to elect, create and sustain creation. God gives a love partner life (or spirit). So from Genesis we receive two important pieces of information about the Spirit: (1) the Spirit gives life, and (2) the Spirit fulfills the purposes of God. The Spirit is the power of God.

The Hebrew understanding of the Spirit advanced as Israel learned of its special destiny as a witness to God before other nations. At several places in the Hebrew story, the Spirit of God comes upon certain individuals—kings, artisans, judges and prophets—to specially equip them for service. And the Holy Spirit is "wild" (Jn 3:5-8); that is, it cannot be manipulated by humans but comes as God desires. Further, the Spirit makes the ordinary sacred for God's purposes. In other words, the Holy Spirit is not merely an enhanced human spirituality. This emphasizes the *uniqueness* and divinity of the Spirit. Through the Spirit human beings (and things) are brought into God's creative and redemptive purposes so that God is glorified and the people of God are edified. In the Hebrew tradition, the Spirit is God's gift of renewal of God's people for God's purposes (Ezek 37:1-14). The Spirit is God's power *and* presence.

The revelation of the Spirit is further expanded with the incarnation and the writing of the New Testament. The incarnation is closely identified with the Spirit's agency (Lk 1:35), and at Jesus' baptism the Spirit fully discloses Jesus' identity, purpose and divinity (Mt 3:16-17; Mk 1:10; Lk 3:21-23). In the Gospels, Jesus' humanity is sustained by the presence of the Spirit, and Jesus unquestionably identifies with the Spirit (Lk 4:14). Unlike the judges, kings and prophets, whom the Spirit visited periodically, Jesus was always uniquely filled by the Spirit (see Lk 10:21). And unlike others under the influence of the Spirit, Jesus is worshiped and accepts the title Lord. Jesus is the Spirit of the Lord in the Hebrew sense—that is, as the Revelation, Will, Helper, Sanctifier, Redeemer and Presence.

This alone is an extensive expansion from the Hebrew tradition on the Spirit. But Jesus added yet another dimension to our understanding of the Spirit, teaching of a Helper or Comforter (Paraclete) for believers. The Spirit's primary role is to teach, testify about Jesus and sustain believers (Jn 14:16-17, 26; 15:26). The Gospel of John in particular adds an entirely personal dimension to the Hebrew understanding of the Spirit: the Spirit now will *remain* with *all* believers to quicken their faithfulness. In the Spirit, God's presence abides with his children.

So, in the biblical tradition two Spirit-related themes emerge. First, the Spirit is a *global* agent, upholding God's purposes in creation itself and in the history of Israel. Second, the Spirit is also a *personal* agent, present within the individual and enabling him or her to know and serve God. And this twofold work is supported in the rest of the New Testament. In the personal sense, the Spirit is working with human agents as they speak of and fulfill God's purposes. In the global sense, the Spirit is the agent of revelation declaring the power of God over creation.

It is important to note that the Spirit's personal work is not antithetical to the global work. The Spirit who works in the individual also sustains creation and moves it to God's glory and purposes. When one aspect is stressed to the exclusion of the other, theological problems arise. The tension between the Spirit's global and personal work erupted very early in Christian theology.

THE POWER OF GOD OR THE PRESENCE OF GOD?

During the first three centuries after Christ's ascension, the church struggled to understand God's triune nature. Several theological positions were developed in response to the challenges of the day. The nature of the Spirit was the last to be examined. Some viewed the Spirit as the power of God; others believed the Spirit was the presence of God. These views effectively made the Spirit a force or mode of God.

The emphasis on the global aspect of the Spirit as the power of God is known as *dynamic monarchianism*. The Spirit is an energy emanating from the Father which allows God's purposes to be achieved in creation. From this perspective, God is a singular entity (monarch), and Jesus is a subservient creature on whom the divine energy (Spirit) imposes the divine will and purposes. There is no incarnation because the Spirit played no role in creating the humanity of Christ. However, Jesus was adopted and animated by the Spirit. Some early Christians felt that this honored the basic Hebrew beliefs about the monotheistic God and the Spirit.

Modalistic monarchianism, on the other hand, stressed God's personal presence in the Spirit. Believing that the Spirit was indeed God in the fullest sense, these Christians thought of the Spirit as a new mode of God in a new era. God first acted as Father and then as Son. Now the Spirit is a new mode of God's interaction with created reality. Modalistic theologies granted that the Spirit was indeed God and is now the primary way God is manifested personally to Christians. The Spirit is not a mere force or energy, but the very presence of God.

In chapter one, we looked at how neither of these options do justice to the personality of the Spirit as presented in the Bible. In order to maintain a strict monotheism, the Spirit is reduced to an emanation, energy or mode of God. But after poring over Scripture and debating for several centuries, the ecumenical church's beliefs about the Trinity and the Spirit were settled at the Councils of Nicaea (325) and Constantinople (381). The Nicene-Constantinopolitan creed (commonly called the Nicene Creed) fully articulates the doctrine of the Spirit. The creed informs us that the Spirit is God, God is Spirit, and the Spirit *is* holy (i.e., not every spirit is God [1 Jn 4:4-6]). Thus the Spirit is not merely an effect or power from God but has the full attributes of God.

The Nicene Creed neatly balances the global (power) and personal (presence) aspects of the Spirit. The Spirit is the "Lord and Giver of life" and is worshiped and glorified along with the Father and Son. Further, the Spirit comforts God's people through the church, baptism and resurrection to a glorious future. Thus the third article of the Nicene Creed begins by placing the Spirit within the triune Godhead and ends by describing the Spirit's presence with the church and individual Christians.

Notice that the Spirit does not move people toward a *private* spirituality. Self-edification and self-fulfillment are not spiritual gifts. Rather, the Spirit lifts creation, collectively and individually, into the life and purposes of God. Life in the Spirit is always for the other, always moving from isolation to community. The Spirit gifts God's creatures to reflect God's triune being, which is the movement of love toward others.

TWO VISIONS OF THE SPIRIT: THE *FILIOQUE* CONTROVERSY

In the eleventh century one of the greatest tragedies in Christian history occurred: the Great Schism between the Eastern and Western branches of the church. In 1054, the patriarch of Constantinople (present-day Istanbul) and the Roman pope excommunicated each other, which inaugurated a split between the Greek-speaking East and the Latin-speaking West. The theological issue concerned different visions of the Holy Spirit that centered on the *filioque* clause added to the Nicene Creed by the Western church.

Originally the third article of the Nicene Creed read, in part: "I believe in the Holy Spirit . . . who proceeds from the Father, who with the Father and the Son together is worshiped and glorified." However, as early as the sixth century, and in official use by 589, the Western tradition had altered the third article to: "I believe in the Holy Spirit . . . who proceeds from the Father *and the Son*, who with the Father and the Son together is worshiped and glorified." The addition of "and the Son" (*filioque* in Latin) created the controversy.

The Latin church added the *filioque* clause because they continued to have conflicts with heresies denying the divinity of Jesus. If the Spirit proceeded from the Father *and* the Son, then it was clear that the Son was indeed equal with the Father. Nonetheless, this simple alteration created theological problems for the Eastern tradition.

To understand what exactly was contested, let's try to visualize "procession." The Latin "double procession" (from Father and Son) is an inverted triangle (bottom-side up). The Father and Son are the two angles at the top of the triangle. The lines proceed from both forming the bottom angle: the Spirit. Now imagine the original Nicene picture. The triangle is the opposite with the Father at the top and the Son and the Spirit at the bottom (see fig. 4.1).

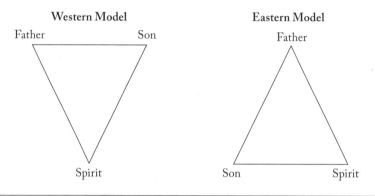

Figure 4.1. Two models of procession within the Trinity

It is unclear which theologian initiated the idea of the double procession. Most scholars point to Augustine of Hippo as the most likely source. He stressed that the Spirit is the manifestation of love between the Father and Son. This can be misunderstood as depersonalizing the Spirit into some sort of spiritual force analogous to the human spirit. If love is Spirit, then any creature capable of love is capable of Spirit.

But there are problems with this way of considering the Spirit. First, the priority falls on the Father and the Son, resulting in a "bi-nity" rather than the trinitarian revelation of God. Further, the Spirit is reduced to a principle—the love inherent in creation—rather than an agent of God's self-revelation and work. This is really more reflective of George Lucas's Jedi "Force" (or Phillip Pullman's "dust") than the Judeo-Christian conception of the personal God. Classically, this position is pantheism: the idea that everything that exists is identical with

God. Creation is itself God. In the trajectory of Augustine's theology, creation is not divine, but love within creation is identical with God.

Further complicating matters, another of Augustine's trinitarian analogies subtly reinforces the depersonalizing of the Spirit. Augustine argued that a "vestige of the Trinity" is found in the human mind, which is composed of *memory* (rationality), *understanding* (judgments or applications of rationality) and *will* (choosing which memories and judgments to act on).

Augustine hoped to demonstrate that when we are Spirit-filled, our wills are aligned with God and we operate in love. So why did this cause so much consternation in the Eastern church? The problem is that Augustine's conception of the will reduces the Spirit to a principle or force without any demarcation of what *particular* Spirit-filled persons should look or act like. The infinite love of God is reduced to a uniform principle: one size fits all. This has two important ramifications.

First, when viewing the Spirit as a power, people speculate about the best kind of receptacle for that power. By the time of the Great Schism, the pope was claiming, in effect, that his office—the bishopric of Rome—was *the* receptacle for this kind of power. Therefore all other bishops and church authorities needed to recognize the supreme authority of Rome. What was an esoteric theological point became a dispute over ecclesial structures of authority. The Roman bishop argued that he was the authoritative receptacle for the operations of the Spirit. He stood in the place of the Spirit. The Eastern bishops, including the patriarch of Constantinople, needed to acquiesce to the authority of God in the papacy. This claim of being not merely "first among equals" but also the sole "vicar of Christ" in terms of authority was unacceptable for the Christians of the Greek-speaking world.

Second, and more subtly, the reduction of the Spirit to a product flattens the individual Christian into a universal type. Individuals are absorbed into the global power or sea of love, and the Trinity as *love in relation* seems to be lost. In opposition to this, the Eastern church offers something else.

In the Eastern tradition the doctrine of the Spirit is that the Spirit is sent, with the Son, from the Father. Since the Son is an accurate reflection of God (remember God is Christlike), so too the Spirit reflects God and shares in the work of the incarnation—God, in other words, is Spiritlike. What this means, in essence, is that in creation and particularly in the Christian the Spirit's task is not to activate some sort of divine capacity in all, but to reveal God as triune and to lift individuals into the life of God so that *each* person's humanity, as envisioned and elected by God, is truly realized. Rather than making us uniform or abstract Christs, the Spirit makes us pneumatic humans—individuals who express our unique purposes in the love of God and therefore extend in service this true and free individuality as relationship to others, just as God has done for us. Sadly, this Spirit-enabled living *for others* is sometimes lost (even in charismatic Christianity).

The Eastern perspective closely reflects the biblical presentation of presence, and it is an important corrective to individualistic spirituality. When the Spirit moves, it does so for *mission* and *service*, not merely for personal enlightenment or benefit. The Spirit frees the human person from sinfulness by offering a vision and reality of God's essential life as love for the other—true humanity. A person living in the Spirit recognizes the presence and work of the Spirit in other Christians, in all other people and even in creation itself.

A THEOLOGY OF THE SPIRIT

British Methodist theologian Geoffrey Wainwright helps us understand the Holy Spirit. Biblically and in the tradition of the church, the Spirit is the constitution and compositor of the Christian church. The Spirit comes corporately and individually in order to *transform* and *enable* Christians to witness and enact God's kingdom. Wainwright notes that this entails four important aspects which are common among all Christian traditions: (1) the Spirit is the power of Christian preaching; (2) the Spirit enables the personal response of faith; (3) the Spirit is sacramentally active as the agent of holiness; and (4) the Spirit is author or source of fellowship.

The first point, the Spirit is the power of Christian preaching, encapsulates a slogan of another Christian theologian, Yves Congar (1904-1995). Congar wrote extensively on the Spirit under the rubric "no Christology without pneumatology, no pneumatology without Christology." This is wonderfully rich and has filled volumes, both by Congar and those who have read him. The basic idea is that the Spirit is sent by the Father in order to reveal Christ. The Spirit ensures a proper understanding of faith, declares Christ, and is the power of God for salvation. God is Christlike, God is Spiritlike, and therefore Christ is Spiritlike. One application of this profound truth is that whenever Christians preach (or witness), it is not the preacher but the Spirit who speaks truthfully. This is wonderfully freeing for anyone who has had the daunting task of preaching.

The second point, the Spirit enables the response of faith, reveals that no one can say Jesus is Lord except by the initiative of the Spirit (1 Cor 12:3). This precludes the Spirit as some sort of spiritual analog to the human spirit. The Spirit does not activate a general human spirituality. Instead, the Spirit convicts humans of sin and opens them to faith, and therefore creates the possibility of a spiritually fulfilling life. Faith stands outside the human person as a gift of God.

For Christians from free church or nonsacramental traditions, Wainwright's third point, the Spirit is the sacramentally active agent of holiness, is hard to understand (see chapter five). For now, it is sufficient to note that sacraments—outward signs of inward realities which God uses to supplement faith—are not made effective by the words or actions of a pastor or priest, but rather the Spirit works through these everyday things (e.g., water, bread and wine). There is nothing special about the words in the Bible or the water in baptism or the bread and wine in Communion *except* that God in the Spirit chooses to work in these things in order to serve God's kingdom. The Spirit's activity, not the object or person, is sacramentally significant.

Finally, the Spirit is author or source of fellowship. The church is neither a building nor a denomination, tradition or merely the communion of the living (see Heb 12:1). Instead, it includes all, dead and alive, who are lifted by God's grace in the Spirit to live for God's purposes. The community of saints comprises those with the common gift of participation in the life of God (2 Cor 13:13), regardless of gifts, ministries, denominations, locations and so forth. Those who have, by the Spirit, joined that pilgrim journey share one Lord, one faith and one baptism (Eph 4). This fellowship is a gift of God and a fruit of the Spirit (Gal 5:22-23). It is the common life of steadily moving toward our sanctification (presence) by the Spirit, which is made possible by God's salvation (power) in Christ. A theology of the Holy Spirit is then a theology of sanctification.

BEING SET ASIDE FOR HOLY PURPOSE

There are surprisingly few theologians, especially in the last few hundred years, who understand Christian life as pneumatic. With the exception of some evangelical and Pentecostal theologians, there has been a resounding silence. With no doctrine of sanctification came the loss of *Christian* ethics.

Up to the Middle Ages, the church had a monopoly on ethics because its offices possessed the Spirit. The church was the culture, and to be a good Catholic was to be Spirit-filled. The Protestant Reformation, however, broke the ancient connection between natural law and divine law as espoused by the church. But the Reformation perspective did not hold. Since the Reformation, the Enlightenment and modern theology have championed the individual and his or her determination of right or wrong. If not conflated with human spirit, the Holy Spirit merely served as a check to outlandish personal preference. Thus the "Spirit-filled" were free individuals making choices without coercion. During this era, though, most people thought and acted with Christian mores and within the Christian ethos because Christianity and the general culture were still so closely allied. The general shape and expectations of Western culture—from government to private citizen—had its roots in Christian ethics. When Christianity and culture are so conflated, proclaiming a radical Christian ethic—that is, being set aside by God for God's purposes—is a difficult task.

As with the Reformation, however, this culture and Christ conflation broke down in the late nineteenth and early twentieth centuries, leading to Karl Barth's "theology in crisis." Notably, we find theologians thinking about sanctification most earnestly in both those periods.

Because the Reformation broke the medieval church-culture hegemony, Martin Luther, his student Philipp Melanchthon (1497-1560) and John Calvin (1509-1564) found they needed to establish a connection between the Word of God and the Spirit, between salvation and good works, and between the individual Christian before God and the individual Christian as God's agent to the wider community. For Luther in the tumultuous 1520s, it was essential to connect justification with sanctification. And John Calvin, a second-generation Reformer, was faced with the perceived failure of the Protestant movement in many cities and towns, and the subsequent retreat back to medieval habits by many Christian people. Justification, for the Reformers, was freedom from not only medieval works righteousness but also the newer antinomian or lawless ethic of the period. Antinomian cults had radical understandings of sanctification, espousing almost any personal preference (from extraordinary asceticism to wild indulgence) as evidence of the fruit of the Spirit. To address these kinds of extremes, Luther, Melanchthon and Calvin needed to think seriously about sanctification and its meaning for the church, individuals and society.

In the early twentieth century Karl Barth saw the devolution of Christian Europe in wars, dictators, growing anti-Semitism, and socioeconomic corruption and abuse. He too spoke of the true freedom found in Christ and the Spirit, but also sought to limit the unmitigated freedom and lawlessness of an entirely personal morality.

The Reformers and crisis theologians turned their attention to the Spirit and the Spirit's role in sanctification. Similarly, evangelicals and

Pentecostals, like the Reformers and crisis theologians, see themselves making a radical break with their culture. The evangelicals, who view themselves as heirs of the Reformation, carefully read the Reformers and try to follow in their footsteps. The Pentecostals believe humanity is literally at the end of the age as prophesied in Joel 2:28-32.

A short definition of sanctification. Sanctification, literally "making holy," comes from the Hebrew Bible and the Jewish tradition of holy ground in the temple's inner room, the holy of holies. This is where the Spirit of God resided. In the Hebrew tradition, objects (and people) are ritually made holy for the purpose of being used in the glorification and worship of God. Anything impure or unholy would be obliterated before the all-consuming glory of God. Therefore to stand before God, God must make an object (Lev 8–9; 1 Kings 7–9) or person (Is 6) holy. Of course, there is also a strong ethical or moral demand placed on Israel as God's elected people. Because Israel's God is holy, by definition, God's people must be holy (Lev 11:44). But due to its sinfulness and folly, Israel repeatedly failed to be holy. However, the gracious God persisted in the salvation and sanctification of Israel. This theme is expanded in the New Testament: "But you were washed, you were sanctified, you were justified in the name of the Lord Jesus Christ and by the Spirit of our God" (1 Cor 6:11).

Sanctification, then, has to do with God, justification and the Holy Spirit. The Spirit transforms and enables us so that we are free to live as partners in peace with God, with each other and in God's creation. We are becoming *pneumatic* humans in the image of the God-man, who was the first truly pneumatic human. "And we, who with unveiled faces all reflect the Lord's glory, are being transformed into his likeness with ever-increasing glory, which comes from the Lord, who is the Spirit" (2 Cor 3:18). Being made holy in the biblical tradition is to be set apart for the purposes of God, to be *that* person in *this* community, who lives free to be God's intended person for *this* place and time.

But is sanctification a once-for-all event, or is it a process? In other words does sanctification come in toto with salvation, or does it grow as a person matures and participates in the common life of the church? To answer this, two theologians are particularly helpful: Calvin and Barth.

John Calvin's double grace. It is possible (and quite common) to misunderstand Luther as stressing the importance of faith or belief itself, rather than Christ. In this account of Luther's theology a person experiences profound anxiety about his or her status before God, and terror sets in because the sinner realizes no amount of good works is sufficient to merit God's approval. In despair, the person has no choice but to blindly cast him- or herself on the promises of God in Christ, which is faith. Only when this faith attaches itself to God does the sinner begin to understand forgiveness (experientially as well as intellectually). Then and only then is the sinner confident that regardless of future actions, the promise of God's forgiveness holds.

The believer's *faith* in those promises, some of Luther's critics argue, saves the sinner, and not God. Critics charge that this entails a twofold sanctification. First, the person is saved and comes to know that he or she is saved. Second, the person then begins to beat down the old sinful nature and adopts more of the new nature won in justification. Faith then is a work by the Christian, whose faith is validated by the change in behavior. God, in other words, is like a parent encouraging an infant to walk, and catching the child when he or she stumbles. Thus the child has faith that he or she will be caught before falling, and this faith allows the child to be bolder in attempting to walk until mastering the skill. Faith is not trusting the parent ("Mommy always catches me") but in the act of walking ("I will not hurt myself").

Despite Luther's best intentions, when sanctification comes into focus in his theology, it is usually a temporal second event in which Christians do something (a work) which validates or reinforces their faith confidence. This faith confidence, however, is not necessarily in God but rather in their commitment. For some, such as John Calvin, this looked like medieval Catholicism's stress on doing what is inside oneself in order to please God or find merit before God. Luther did really well with the beginning of salvation—justification—but Calvin thought the rest of the story was left ambiguous.

To address this, Calvin roots justification and sanctification more centrally in the covenant and the lordship of Christ. Justification and sanctification, for Calvin, do not rest on faith but in the faithfulness of faith's object—God. With the Christian's incorporation into Christ, the Christian is made holy objectively in God. So justification and sanctification are a simultaneous double unfolding (double grace) of the objective promise. Faith is the working out of our radically new justified existence in obedience to the Holy Spirit's work on the human will. Faith then is not a prerequisite. For Calvin, the Holy Spirit's sanctifying work is not merely internal (as in Luther) but very much public and communal. Hearing and reading the Word and participating in church life are locations of the Spirit's sanctifying activity.

John Calvin helps us understand that the *person* and *work* of the Spirit are outcomes of the trinitarian work of God. On account of Christ's work Christians receive complete forgiveness, full justification or "mystical union" with Christ, in which the fullness of Christ is given to the Christian. For Calvin, the Spirit does not merely confirm a person's faith but actually effects the union between Christ and the Christian. Faith is the result of, not the prerequisite for, being in Christ. The Spirit is at the very center of the Christian life, and the Spirit shapes that life as it is called to the work of God. Thus there is a demand that Christian life look different, shaped by the gospel reality personally and communally. The Christian community must be congruent with Christian principles. For Calvin, the Sermon on the Mount and other biblical admonitions weren't things to be aspired toward, they were to be absolutely fulfilled through the Spirit.

This changes the illustration of the infant learning to walk. Now, because of the love of the parent, the child has faith in the parent and not in the act of walking.

Karl Barth's Spirit of promise. According to Calvin, God in the Spirit is the agent of salvation, and faith is the proper human *response* to salvation. Calvin expected (demanded?) the development of habitual

Christian virtues as a fruit of sanctification. Following Calvin's trajectory, some later theologians, such as John Wesley, argued that moral or sinless perfection is the final evidence of salvation. The idea that sin could persist in someone made holy by God was ludicrous. Hence, some Christians consider complete sanctification as evidence of the truly elect. Christians, who are indeed holy, are now armed to resist all sin. In essence, sin is not an issue for sanctified Christians. Is there a problem with this?

Well, for one thing the list of true Christians would be very short! In correcting Luther, Calvin stressed the singularity of justification and sanctification. Thus sanctification would be understood as a one-time event. It can also lead to an understanding that holiness, which is properly God's, is now a de facto human possession (even though divinely gifted). This appears to be a forceful expulsion of human personality in favor of a new perfection; the Christian individual is overwritten by the Spirit into something new and different. The old person is radically morphed into a new person. This begs the question of whether the individual Christian is actually important to God. Fortunately, Karl Barth's writings on the Spirit add an important dimension to Calvin, which he learned from Luther!

Both Calvin and Barth thought of the Spirit from a trinitarian perspective. Calvin primarily begins with the Spirit as Reconciler between God and humanity, and deduces that what cannot be properly present in God (sin) must not be present in the redeemed sinner. Calvin therefore concludes that sanctification and justification are simultaneous. Redemption depends on the Spirit reconciling two impossible states: sin and holiness. After this reconciliation, the Spirit reveals (Revealer) and reinforces (Redeemer) that activity. Barth flips the argument and starts with the Spirit as Redeemer, who in that activity reveals God as the Reconciler who declares a "now" and "not yet" that is becoming true for each Christian. As Redeemer the Spirit *promises* something that is ultimate, final and future, and paradoxically, has a starting point in human existence as both sinful and justified. The point for Barth was to illustrate that this is still a radical difference between Spirit and human spirit as piety not only in terms of kind (e.g., we are not in the process of becoming the Spirit) but also even in quality or time itself. Nonetheless, it is still something "be-coming" for us because of God's work. As Redeemer, Barth notes, the Spirit gives something that creatures cannot attain, and therefore reveals (1) who God really is as Creator, Redeemer and Sanctifier, and (2) who humanity is as created, redeemed and sanctified.

Thus there is a tension in terms of who/what we seemingly are and who/what we really are. Barth does not want to argue that we are in the process of becoming divine or that we will be something completely different through the work of the Spirit. But he does alert us to a tension. But this tension is overcome by the revelation of God's trustworthiness and character, because God elects to reveal to us as Redeemer in the Spirit. For Barth, God as Redeemer declares the uniqueness of Spirit and therefore of God. As Redeemer, God comes in reality *and* in promise, as a future certainty won solely in, by and through God, which cannot be thwarted by human folly or sin. This is our hope. Of course, hope is not wishful thinking or human optimism. Hope is belief in the trustworthiness of the Agent of transformation, even in the midst of our sinful, groaning state. Barth cleverly notes that as heirs we are not possessors but those to whom possession is promised, and that promise is sustained by the nearness of God.

Barth states that the life of the Christian is a "life lived in hope." The "Christliness of the Christian life" is our sanctification, which produces a desire to please God, a Christian conscience as the Christian participates in the ways the Spirit reveals God to humanity. This revelation most notably comes by participation in the Christian community (church) and in the Word and sacrament—modes by which Christ (or the Spirit of Christ) is made present and our hope is actualized through works. Second, Christian life produces gratitude, thankfulness and worship, and thus our deeds slowly begin to match our reality declared in Christ. We learn that the circumscribed freedom of being a child of

God means that when we follow God's revelation, we are open to obedience to the One whose love is so compelling, and nothing detrimental is found there. Thankfulness and worship are fruits of the Spirit. Finally, Barth tells us, true prayer is made in the Spirit. We speak boldly with our Father, realizing that our right to speak to God is made possible by the Spirit, who re-creates us as children of God. The Spirit enables us to tell God the truth about ourselves—sinful and needy—because the Spirit also tells us who God is, our Redeemer. Barth neatly summarizes this point: "It has pleased God to take this groaning, sighing person, with his burden, upon Himself."[1]

Let's return once more to the infant learning to walk. Barth suggests this pattern. Each time the child stumbles or falls, he or she experiences the parent's protection and expects the same in the future. Therefore the child tries again. The child learns mommy's character ("She helps me to walk") and also hopes in mommy ("She will catch me"), so the confident child indeed learns to walk. Barth reintroduces into Luther's and Calvin's doctrines of sanctification the parent's persistent presence and saving action that enables the child to grow into the parent's expectation.

SUMMING UP

The doctrine of the Spirit is a Christian necessity. It is not merely for Pentecostals or charismatics. Nor is it simply about "signs and wonders" or speaking in tongues. In Scripture and Christian tradition, the Spirit is God's power and comforting presence for the people of God. In the Spirit we become not only our true selves but also relationally open and active to others in love. The Spirit is therefore the shape of Christian life. But as the *filioque* controversy teaches us, there is not one uniform shape or model. Instead, the Spirit brings about Christlikeness (pneumatic humans) in each Christian, helps Christians recognize the Spirit in others and in creation, creates a new community and ethic of the

---

[1]Karl Barth, *The Holy Spirit and the Christian Life: The Theological Basis of Ethics*, trans. R. Birch Hoyle (Louisville, Ky.: Westminster John Knox Press, 1993), p. 68.

coming kingdom of God, and guides Christians as they live out their sanctification as intended by the triune God.

No Christian tradition can ignore pneumatology. Come, Holy Spirit!

DISCUSSION QUESTIONS

1. In your own words, explain the relationship between the Holy Spirit's global power and personal presence in the Christian life.

2. Define sanctification in your own words.

3. Recalling the *filioque* controversy, which do you think to be more important: to be a "Christ" or to be "Christ-like"? Is there a difference in the Holy Spirit's agency?

BIBLIOGRAPHY

Introductory

Anderson, Allan. *An Introduction to Pentecostalism: Global Charismatic Christianity.* New York: Cambridge University Press, 2004. Pentecostal.

Bruner, Frederick Dale. *A Theology of the Holy Spirit: The Pentecostal Experience and the New Testament Witness.* Grand Rapids: Eerdmans, 1970. Presbyterian.

Green, Michael. *I Believe in the Holy Spirit.* Grand Rapids: Eerdmans, 1975. Evangelical Anglican.

Welker, Michael, ed. *The Work of the Spirit: Pneumatology and Pentecostalism.* Grand Rapids: Eerdmans, 2006. Pentecostal.

Intermediate

Barth, Karl. *The Holy Spirit and the Christian Life.* 1938. Reprint, Philadelphia: John Knox, 1993. Reformed.

Berkouwer, G. C. *Faith and Sanctification.* Grand Rapids: Eerdmans, 1952. Reformed.

Congar, Yves. *The Word and Spirit.* San Francisco: Harper & Row, 1984. Roman Catholic.

Jenson, Robert. *The Triune Identity: God According to the Gospels*. Philadelphia: Fortress, 1982. Lutheran.

Moltmann, Jürgen. *The Spirit of Life: A Universal Affirmation*. Philadelphia: Fortress, 1992. Reformed.

Taylor, John. *The Go-Between God: The Holy Spirit and Christian Mission*. London: SCM, 1972. Anglican.

Advanced

Badcock, Gary. *Light of Truth and Fire of Love*. Grand Rapids: Eerdmans, 1997. Evangelical Anglican.

Bulgakov, Sergius. *The Wisdom of God*. New York: Paisley, 1937. Orthodox.

Burns, J. P., and G. Fagin. *The Holy Spirit*. Wilmington, Del.: Michael Glazier, 1984. Roman Catholic.

Wainwright, Geoffrey. *Doxology: The Praise of God in Worship, Doctrine and Life: A Systematic Theology*. Oxford: Oxford University Press, 1980. Methodist.

Yong, Amos. *Spirit-Word-Community: Theological Hermeneutics in Trinitarian Perspective*. Surrey, U.K.: Ashgate, 2002. Pentecostal.

5

THE DOCTRINES OF
THE BIBLE AND SACRAMENTS

"From infancy you have known the holy Scriptures, which are able
to make you wise for salvation through faith in Christ Jesus. All
Scripture is God-breathed and is useful for teaching, rebuking,
correcting and training in righteousness, so that the man of God
may be thoroughly equipped for every good work."

2 TIMOTHY 3:15-17

UNLIKE THE FIRST FOLLOWERS OF JESUS, most of today's Christians have never set eyes on Jesus of Nazareth, heard his words directly or witnessed his death and resurrection. Most of today's Christians were not in that little room when the Holy Spirit inaugurated the church (Acts 2), and yet one out of three persons in the world is identified as Christian.

This chapter examines how Christ is present in the Spirit to the community of faith by the mediating grace of the Bible as the Word of God and the sacraments as the presence of God. Taking a middle line between highly sacramental and nonsacramental theology, I argue that both the Scripture and sacraments are vehicles in which Christ is made objectively and personally present. Word and sacrament are witnesses to the reality of God, who declares, redeems and sustains humans for life lived before and in worship of God (2 Tim 4:1-5).

In making Christ known, does God work *only* through the Bible and sacraments? No. But God consistently and in divine freedom chooses to manifest grace through these. It is a witness to the love and grace of God that mere words and objects are used by God to create a people of praise and mission.

In most systematic theologies the Bible and sacraments would fall under the rubric of the church (this is, after all, where they are found). I have chosen to treat them separately for two reasons. They address (in part) (1) how we can know Christ *now*, and (2) the nature of God's life that we are being lifted into. Certainly, we are being lifted into the church as a taste of the coming kingdom, but the means of God's grace—how these are created and normalized—are the Bible and sacraments.

MAKING CHRIST PRESENT: THE BIBLE

Every year, I ask ordinands—those seeking to become ministers of the gospel—and third-year systematic-theology students the same two questions: Have you formulated a theology of the Bible? and Can you relate that theology to a theology of preaching? Over the years there hasn't been one student who could articulate an adequate answer. This is both surprising and not surprising to me.

It is surprising because throughout their entire calling, ministers will preach from the Bible. This raises some serious questions: What do they think they will be doing with that text? And why is the Bible special? Why not use some poem, popular book, movie or personal anecdote in the place of the Bible? Properly answering these questions requires a theology of Scripture.

But I am also not surprised because biblical, theological and pastoral studies are bifurcated. Thus homiletic studies focus more on rhetorical form and technique than the theological foundations of preaching. Admittedly, the need to be a good communicator is important. And this emphasis is part of the problem, but the wedge between biblical and theological studies is more troubling. The result is that the theology of Scripture and preaching are seldom integrated.

In this chapter I suggest that the Bible, like the sacraments, is a mediating grace. This means that through the Bible the real presence of Christ (or the Spirit of God) is manifest to the people of God, overcoming sin in the life of the individual Christian and shaping the Christian community as witnesses to the reality of God. There is nothing magical about the Bible. But God's grace makes the ordinary words (thoughts, records and histories) of Scripture something extraordinary.

A DISCOVERY OF HISTORY

Historian and religious studies scholar Philip Jenkins relates a tale told by African theologian Musimbi Kanyoro. When 2 Corinthians 13:14—"May the grace of the Lord Jesus Christ, and the love of God, and the fellowship of the Holy Spirit be with you all"—was read to a Kenyan church, the entire Christian community responded with "Thank you, Paul." For the Kenyan congregation, Paul was actually present with them. This kind of response would be unlikely in a Western congregation.

This illustrates that a shift—the discovery of history—has occurred in the Western world, and we take this shift for granted and never question it. The discovery of history emerged in philosophical circles around A.D. 1700, when European Christian culture was under siege. Two hundred years earlier, Western Christianity had splintered into Roman Catholic and Protestant streams, and Protestantism split even further into factions. Europe had engaged in numerous religious wars, causing people to question the truth of Christianity itself. Intellectuals were growing skeptical about any kind of learning. Skepticism's roots go all the way back to ancient Greek philosophy. It held that there could be no certain knowledge of anything, no real truth and that everything was relative. What is true for one person is not necessarily true for another. But most people instinctively knew skepticism was no foundation for a civil society.

At about the same time, Europe entered a great age of discovery. New lands and laws of nature were constantly being uncovered. The mysteries of God, it seemed, were being exposed through science and mathematics, which seemed to some to be the answer to Europe's religious strife and intellectual skepticism. Civil life, personal morality and even religion itself could be based on mathematical or scientific laws. Natural philosophers—the ancestor of today's laboratory scientist—looked for "common places" (universal truths) on which to build certain knowledge of everything.

The rise of a form of a *mathematical* certainty worried many. Consider the work of the great physicist Isaac Newton (1642-1727) whose experiments explained the most mysterious thing of all—light itself, which had always been equated with God. Likewise all over Western Europe, scholars were busy applying mathematics to phenomena they observed in the heavens (astronomy) and in the earth (chemistry, biology and physics). This was a great departure from the system of scientific inquiry that had held for nearly two thousand years.

The influence of the Greek philosopher Aristotle (384-322 B.C.) on the church, seen in the theology of Thomas Aquinas, recently had been rejected by the Protestant Reformers. And Aristotle's astronomy (specifically his geocentrism) was being overturned by the astronomical observations of Johannes Kepler (1571-1630) and Galileo Galilei (1564-1642). But what was really being rejected by these scientists was Aristotle's assumption that *thinking* about something was more important than *observing* it. Thus, for example, gravity did not need to be tested because Aristotle had already explained gravity as the propensity for an object to seek its natural "love" for its place. It stood to reason, therefore, that two objects, one heavier than another, would fall at different rates of speed. Bigger objects would fall faster than lighter objects. Nevertheless, Galileo disproved Aristotle with his famous Tower of Pisa experiments, trumping centuries of errant thinking through experimentation and observation.

The scientific revolution produced an epistemological paradigm shift—empiricism—which fundamentally altered Western civilization. Empiricists believe one central truth: certain knowledge is attained by experience alone. Nothing is certain until it is experienced publicly and then explained mathematically. In our scientific world, this seems obvious, but for the early modern world it was earth-shaking. Much of what was thought to be certain—believed on the basis of reason and authority—came under suspicion, including the truths of Christianity.

Empiricism maintains that any "truth" that cannot be verified by public experience and scientific observation must be rejected. *Experience* is not defined as what is meaningful to an individual but what is accessible and knowable to all, under the same conditions. This is troubling to two kinds of people. First, religious (or poetic) people who accept that there is much that cannot be explained empirically, including beauty, love and God. Second, philosophers who believe that the human mind is more than a blank slate onto which experiences are inscribed. According to the latter, known as rationalists, the certainty the empiricist desires is impossible without the mind's rational process of organizing observations and experiences.

Rationalists argue that the mind shuttles back and forth from experience to thought and thought to experience, which permits certain types of scientific, mathematical knowledge. Further, without the active rational mind, human beings are not capable of freely choosing their behavior, and instead would be merely instinctive creatures, well-trained, unthinking apes.

What would happen in a world in which actions are not choices but merely the "environment acting out"? For a moral philosopher the implication is that no legal system could hold people accountable. We could do only what is in our nature. For the rationalist, empiricism, while promising much, is painted into a metaphysical and scientific corner. It is true that we know from experience, but it is also true that the knower contributes or organizes knowledge. Further, the mind also makes choices; thus ethics are necessary. Animals are not morally culpable, because they work with experience and instinct. But humans make choices and are rewarded or punished on the basis of those choices, which is the foundation of our civil life.

In his *Critiques,* written between 1781 and 1790, Immanuel Kant attempted to bridge the empiricist-rationalist divide with a hybrid movement called *idealism.* Idealism holds that there is indeed a correspondence between experience (empiricism) and the active human mind (rationalism). Thoughts and experience are organized in the human mind as necessary ideas (mirroring God's own infinite and organized mind), which create human knowledge and certainty.

For our purposes idealism's significance is twofold. First, God is a unique entity and the warrant for human uniqueness. Being a Spirit, God cannot be experienced like any other kind of being. But we must think of God as giving order to the world and our minds lest we fall into a continual doubt. God is one of the necessary ideas of the mind. To explain this, consider how we know an object in time and space. We experience an event or object (e.g., this book) and our minds categorize the experience in terms of time (now) and space (here). But *now* and *here* are not a part of the object itself—they belong to our mind; they are ideas within our mind which we think about. But they are not part of our experience. God is also like time and space—something we think about, but not in a way that we think of anything else. God, according to Kant, is "unthinkable" in any ordinary sense. Thus God, for some after Kant, is known through feeling or the sense of awe rather than in reasoned terms. God becomes our spirit.

Second, and more pertinent to our story, is that the human person is the sole arbiter of reality. If I cannot know it, understand it, organize it and explain it—then it is not real, valid or even true. Everything flows through my own interpretation because I am intrinsically set up to be just that—an accurate interpreter. This has profound significance when we come to think about history, events and ourselves.

Here's an illustration to help us understand this rather abstract point. In almost every major art museum there are paintings depicting scenes from the Bible. In most paintings created before the modern era, the central characters are almost always dressed according to the painter's perception of the biblical period or according to a readily accepted archetype that everyone would recognize. (As an example of a modern archetype, think about William Shatner wearing a Starfleet uniform as Captain Kirk.) There is a publicly accepted image of the character; that is, the central biblical characters are presented in that archetypal costume. However, and most crucially, the noncentral characters are usually portrayed in clothes and habits contemporary to the artist. These stand outside the historical archetypes associated with the central figures. Two "histories" are therefore depicted in the same painting: (1) the archetypal biblical period, and (2) the contemporary period of the artist. And by examining the artistic shift in the depiction of biblical times we begin to understand how our view of history had changed from premodern to modern times.

In modern paintings of biblical scenes, care is taken to be historically accurate; if someone contemporary is painted into the scene, that person is pictured in the historical context as a real-time observer. For example, to be historically accurate as possible *The Passion of the Christ* (2004) was filmed using the (now dead) languages spoken at the time of Christ. And when producer-director Mel Gibson wanted to be in the film, he did so as a Roman soldier nailing Jesus to the cross. This tells us something about how we, and modernity, understand history.

Modernity, following the idealist synthesis of rationalism and empiricism, came to understand history as both an inner and outer reality. History is a series of facts that are external to us. However, those facts are not random but are organized by humans to make sense. The human mind does this, creating order of the external world. In this sense the mind discovers history. The first great proponent of the discovery of history was Gotthold Ephraim Lessing (1729-1781). Lessing had a problem with the Christian tradition that the Bible was revelation from God *and* a human work. Lessing had little difficulty with the second half: the Bible, for him, was a series of human writings; some were of great historical and moral value, but others seemed questionable or completely preposterous. As pointed out by Hermann Samuel Reimarus (1694-1768), there were multiple instances in which the Bible contradicted either itself or known history. If it were divine revelation, surely God would have done better work. Lessing felt that this alone was enough to reject the Bible as a document that accurately reported history. There was, however, a more substantial problem to be dealt with.

Lessing's primary problem with the Bible concerned the inner reality of history. Even were it to be found historically trustworthy, Lessing believed that the Bible's miracles, including the resurrection of Jesus Christ, made it ahistorical (or antihistorical). For Lessing, the jumble of information that we encounter as history only makes sense when there is some principle of conformity operative between the events of history and the historian. Just as Kant's philosophy created a bridge between experience and reason, so must there be a similar bridge between "then" (historical data) and "now" (our understanding or reasoned account). The bridge, he concluded, is reason itself. Thus to cross the ditch of particularity (any event in history), we need the bridge of reason.

Through reason, historians can, in effect, travel through time and insert themselves into the past event they are observing, not as subjective interpreters but as certain and objective actors in the scene (remember our painting illustrations). Our sense of history then is necessarily detached from our experience of history.

Back to Mel Gibson and his film. His subjective reason for participating in Jesus' crucifixion scene is not history. In interviews Gibson said because he is a sinner, he believes he nailed Jesus to the cross, so he wanted to participate in the scene. Gibson thought that his subjective feeling could be validated by the historical event. But here is the rub: in traveling backward in time Gibson took himself out of the subjective experience that he tried to set up. He truly thinks his sin is part of the reason for Jesus' death, and he wants to be one of the soldiers nailing Jesus to the cross. But in order to experience that inner reality, he was compelled to become a Roman soldier and not Mel Gibson. The *his-*

torical answer to who nailed Jesus to the cross (Roman soldiers acting under orders) is different from the *theological* answer (me as a sinner).

Despite our intrinsic desire to attach meaning to events, our discovery of history limits the effectiveness of that desire. What Gibson wanted was a theologically informed experience; what he created was a different historical reality. In real history, it was a soldier who nailed Jesus to the cross and not today's sinners.

As Lessing looked at the Bible, he saw that it is both valuable and problematic. It is valuable in that many people have learned from and prospered by its teachings, particularly the ethical teachings of Jesus. However, it has two problems. First, the Bible is full of miracles, and by definition a miracle is not a natural event or part of everyday experience. The miraculous cannot be the foundation for universal truth because it is not a universal experience. It is extraordinary and unrepeatable. Thus any biblical event that has a miracle attached to it cannot, by definition, be a *historical* event. It is not so much that it did not happen, but that we cannot know with certainty that it did happen and therefore cannot apply it to our situation. Contrast a miraculous event with the history of Julius Caesar. We can learn from Caesar's rise and fall because he was a mere human, like us. Through him we can see how power, greed, love and so forth interacted with the sociopolitical realities of his time. Through reason we can re-create Caesar and judge him accordingly. We float above the events with a bird's-eye view, seeing everything at once. And we can apply what we learn to our lives.

Because miracles are ahistorical, much of the Bible's authority fades away. The miraculous accounts of God's interaction with Israel and Jesus have to be removed from the canon of history. When the miraculous is removed, only the ethical or moral dimensions of Jesus and the Hebrew Bible remain. Universal principles of ethical behavior are sought beneath the stories of miracles. Thus, for example, the miraculous feeding of the multitudes by Jesus (Mk 6:30-44; 8:1-13) from a few loaves and fishes becomes a story about sharing what we have, even if meager, with others. Thus, reason makes miracles sensible.

Lessing's second problem with the Bible is more oblique and harder to understand. Many of the theologians of Lessing's time advocated the plenary inspiration of Scripture; that is, the original autographs of the Bible, being fully inspired by God, were without error. But Lessing had read Reimarus's work on the historical and scientific errors in the Bible, and he concluded that the Bible could not be the product of a perfect God. It had to be strictly human in origin. But what drove those authors to write, to invent miracles and to distort the facts? We need to peel away the miracle and distortions to find the kernel of truth in the husk of the story. This is the task of the interpreter.

In modern biblical scholarship, there are thus two perspectives from which to understand the Bible: by bypassing history or by embracing history.

The first stance—bypassing history—finds personal or existential meaning in the Bible. While historical questions may be asked of the Bible, those questions are important only as aids to the existential application of the Bible to the individual. The reader makes the connections from "then" to "now," acting as the bridge between history and the self. The reader looks below the surface of the historical events to find their meaning and posits that meaning (then) as analogous to his or her meaning (now). The scene, language and time may be different, but in both cases humans have the same kinds of needs, fears, hopes, dreams and spirituality.

Actually, the reader begins with the need and then works backward to the text to fulfill the need. For example, perhaps someone longs to be accepted, faults and all. This need is met in the stories about Jesus and the forgiveness of sin. It is not necessary for Jesus to be the divine Son of God (a miracle); instead he stands as an avatar of a spiritual truth. Note that the *observer* adjudicates meaning; the "now" gives the "then" its meaning. As such, history is a chimera or oasis for our needs. It is *our* history, not the history of facts that we interpret. Contrary to Lessing's hope that this view of history would be reasonable and impartial, it is not impartial at all.

The second stance in contemporary biblical studies is to embrace history. In this case, underneath the surface of the text of the Bible lie competing agendas. The Bible is the product of a series of authors, editors and commentators who added, corrected or overwrote the predecessors' work. This editing by each was done to gain advantage within their community. The text of the last editor was accepted by the community as the final authority. But the text still bears telltale signs of the previous authors and editors. Understanding the history of these sublayers is the key to history. Biblical scholars attempt to peel away the interests, needs and histories of the competing voices beneath the text in order to establish the history of its composition and therefore the power hidden in the text.

In this case, the scholar examines the entire history of a text, using the tools of archaeology and literary theory to uncover the voices submerged beneath the surface. But this view of history encounters Lessing's ditch between "now" and "then." Though it claims to be impartial and objective, its historical method is riddled with subjectivity and bias. Histories, even those coming out of the Western academy, do not have a privileged position of objectivity. Historical objectivity, which has been a prevailing myth in the Western academy, is fast losing its credibility. Our global peers have made us aware that as we read history, we also make it.

Now, let's return to our original illustrations. In the case of premodern (and now postmodern) paintings, the fact that peripheral characters remain in their contemporary clothing is a concession that there is an uncrossable gap between "then" and "now." Thus a sixteenth-century Flemish man in a biblical scene remains a sixteenth-century Flemish man. The biblical event has meaning, but it is meaning for "now." Likewise, when Paul sends out his greetings and the Kenyan congregation responds to him in real time, the Kenyans are engaged in something other than a historical reconstruction. Paul is meeting them in their Kenyan context, and they are meeting Paul as Kenyans that morning. History has little to do with it, and this has great theological significance.

I believe that the ditch between the past and present is overcome by the Spirit, who makes Christ present. The Spirit grants meaning to the Bible and sacraments. Just as God overcomes human folly in the incarnation—creating something new and truly real for each human—so the Spirit, through the Bible and sacraments, overcomes human folly to work out God's purposes. The homogenous principle that Lessing sought to bridge "then" and "now" is the *homogeneity of God's character* and self-revelation. God overcomes historical follies, even sinfulness, making finite humans and their actions serve God's purposes. The Bible as Scripture becomes a means of grace.

A THEOLOGY OF SCRIPTURE

In developing a theology of Scripture (and sacraments) we need to avoid two cardinal errors: (1) ascribing to an object what is properly a property of God, and (2) reducing God's revelation to human insight. The first error leads to bibliolatry—the worship of the Bible because the powers and character of God are falsely attributed to it. The Bible is perceived to be nearly magical and often is used as a way of manipulating or invoking God.

In the second error, Scripture becomes the best example of human attempts to capture the mystery of the divine. Over millennia its language has proved more valuable in expressing human spirituality and insight than most human literature, and is one of a small group of religiously useful texts.

How do we navigate between these two extremes?

Overcoming modernity's unthinkability of God. German theologian Eberhard Jüngel (1934-) proposes that modernity has taken a long flight into the "unthinkability of God," which is confused with God not being present at all. When Jüngel speaks of God as being "unthinkable" or "placeless" he means that God in the Judeo-Christian tradition, unlike other gods or deities, is not at human disposal, invocation or manipulation. The Judeo-Christian God is a totally free Other. But through the incarnation God has chosen to be bound to creation in order to sanctify it through the work of the Spirit. Jüngel reminds us that the *triune* God, despite difference, is in the business of speaking and revealing. That *kind* of God assumes matter in order to speak, which enables us to speak as well as think about God.

God's self-revelation then is necessary if humans are to say or know anything about God, because God is not a function of human spirit or of creation itself, but remains without place—namely, unsignified (without analogy) or supranatural. With Jüngel, we have a starting point in developing a theology of Scripture and sacraments. Unless God speaks, no "thing" (nothing) is able to carry within itself any information about or semblance to God. Jüngel calls this "God's more than necessity." This "more than necessity," in terms of God's self-revelation, is the very fact that no thing can, in itself, signify or bear God, and therefore God's revelation is an ontological shock—a miracle, an event outside human expectation and beyond manipulation. God is indeed unthinkable, but God wants us to think about God and enables this in a miraculous manner. God's revelation is always outside of human control, even in the Bible and the sacraments themselves. In other words, the Bible is ordinary, but God working through it is extraordinary, the ontological shock of God.

Jüngel offers three interesting propositions about why God might want to be "placed" or thought about, despite being, by definition, placeless: (1) humanity and its world are interesting for their own sake; (2) God is interesting for his own sake; and (3) God makes humanity, which is interesting in its own sake, interesting in a new way. Understanding these is critical to developing a robust doctrine of revelation and a theology of Scripture and sacraments.

In the first proposition, Jüngel informs us that the created world and humanity are important in their own right; they are not merely a dress rehearsal for a future existence. Our present is part of God's intended purposes for humanity and creation. In metaphysical terms, Jüngel tells us that matter (creation and temporal—even sinful—creatures) matters to God. In biblical terms, creation is "good" (Gen 1:31). Therefore we should not be surprised that God is interested in creation and calls us to live in creation as a people of God.

In the second proposition, Jüngel tells us that God is indeed the source of everything and that no "thing" (nothing) exists in its truest purpose without being connected to its source and origin. In metaphysical terms, God is the highest good, and everything created by God will be brought, by God's persistent and loving action, into relationship with God. In biblical terms, God does not wish for creation to be alone (Gen 1:26). But it is Jüngel's final proposition that opens a theology of revelation and permits a theology of Scripture and sacrament.

In the third proposition, we learn what the doctrines of the Trinity, incarnation and Spirit already taught us: God has not left the world alone but finds ways and means to overcome the world's hostility, indifference and even very materiality. This makes propositions one and two interrelated, which means that humanity and creation share in God's own life. In short, God determines to be "God for humanity" and humanity is declared to be "humanity for God." God therefore finds ways to speak, fulfill and sanctify humanity. This is what the Bible and sacraments do—they mediate grace or God's pleasure for humanity and creation. In so doing, God takes something ordinary (as in the incarnation) and lifts (assumes) it to the divine for the purposes of God.

Jüngel proposes that the Bible is "apostolic" speech and is an "analogy of event" in which God "makes use of the obvious in the world in such a way that God proves God to be that which is even more obvious over and against the mundane."[1] This essentially means that God ceases to be alone, introducing God's own self with God's coming or revelation. This coming, however, is part of God's very being of love, which is exhibited in the ordinary (of which Jesus is the most ordinary in terms of being *fully* human). But in coming, literally *over*coming, in the ordinary or mundane, God proves God's own uniqueness. Only God

---

[1]Eberhard Jüngel, *God as the Mystery of the World*, trans. Darrell L. Guder (Grand Rapids: Eerdmans, 1983), p. 285.

could pull off the miracle of using words and objects to tell us about God. Further, this coming establishes its own grounds of correspondence—it is defined by God's usage and not by human manipulation or action. God comes on God's own terms. Finally, it means that verification of this event is not the task of theology. Christian theology's task is learning to hear what God says because God always says yes to enabling our speech about God to form us to God's pleasure. Or in more biblical terms:

> As surely as *God is faithful*, our message to you is not "Yes" and "No." For the Son of God, Jesus Christ, who was preached among you by me and Silas and Timothy, was not "Yes" and "No," but in him it has always been "Yes." For no matter how many promises God has made, *they are "Yes" in Christ*. And so through him the "Amen" is spoken by us to the glory of God. Now it is *God who makes* both us and you *stand firm in Christ*. He *anointed* us, set his seal of ownership on us, and *put his Spirit in our hearts* as a deposit, guaranteeing what is to come. (2 Cor 1:18-22, italics added)

Jüngel alerts us to the idea that Scripture's witness to the Word of God is an entirely different and particular form of communication than humans had previously or naturally considered or encountered. It is a unique "theology of language" because of its Object. And therefore, *Scripture has a unique nature*. It is both ordinary human words, contextualized in their situation and milieu, and God speaking to God's people the enduring yes of God. Theology's task, for Jüngel, is working out that unique coherence, not treating Scripture as merely another human book but rather as God's speech. This means leaving behind centuries of modernity.

A God who invites (Mt 22:1-14). Jüngel helps us understand that a robust doctrine of revelation—God's willingness to interact with humans and tell us about God—grounds any reflection on Scripture (and sacraments).[2] This means that theological talk about Scripture

---

[2]In my opinion the finest theologian to write on Scripture in the last thirty years or so has to

and sacraments is a reflection on the activity of the triune God, who freely discloses God's being and ways to creatures as part of the saving economy of divine mercy. A theology of Scripture is concerned with the *identity* of the self-manifesting God. It tells us about who God is. This means

1. Revelation is an event or mode of relation. It is God's speaking.

2. Efficacy (and perspicuity) is guaranteed by divine self-action. These are old terms used to convey that Scripture does its job to convict of sin (its efficacy) and to give the comfort of salvation (its perspicuity) and is adequate to those jobs alone.

3. Revelation is a history of divine fellowship: a fellowship that is divinely initiated even with and in human sin and human processes. God is the "Overcomer" of sin and human processes always and forever.

4. Revelation is reconciliation, wherein God overcomes that which hinders humanity from fellowship.

5. Scripture is a function of God's speaking—constructed to reveal the triune reality of God's self-manifestation and orientated to this purpose. Scripture and the words therein is (are) not "reifications"—bits of "God in text"—but realities (words) used by God toward the church/world and from which the church learns to confess that lordship.

6. Scripture, then, is apostolic. As apostolic, it is also human in that human minds and hands are used by God in order to witness to God's purposes.

This has several implications for our theology of Scripture, which again run contrary to modern minds. First, the mode of hearing or reception is obedience (e.g., prayer and worship) rather than judgment as practiced in the historical method. We make judgments to be certain of what God is saying, but first we must learn to hear and to obey. Second,

---

be John B. Webster, formerly of the Oxford University and now at the University of Aberdeen (see *Holy Scripture: A Dogmatic Sketch* [New York: Cambridge University Press, 2003]). Most of what follows I learned from him.

revelation may also mean a *Deus absconditus* (the hiddenness of God), a hiddenness that reflects our *hope* in God alone so that no one owns the Scripture or controls access or interpretation of it as a function of either office, role or other human means. Sometimes, we need to stop speaking about Scripture in order to do what it mandates in the hope that further understanding will come as the church is faithful. Our hope—God's hiddenness wherein we cannot control or conjure God at our need—means that we are forced to trust God's goodness rather than *our* sense of what or whether God might be.

This implies that Scripture is a witness to God (i.e., a means of grace). In this instance, the notion of witness carries with it the assertion that Scripture is a human reality annexed by divine use. It is *divine* use, not human use that has determined the texts to be Scripture. The texts are *appointed* to become instrumental means of gracious divine action. They are, dogmatically speaking, sanctified—that is, loaned *(sanctitas aliena)* the glory of God *(sanctitas positiva)* for the purposes of God.

As such, they have an authority, the acknowledgement by the church "that the church is not left to itself in proclamation" (Barth). Contrary to someone like Dan Brown or modern historians, the church does not find some texts to be better than others and designate them as Scripture. Instead, we must begin by understanding that the church comprises those called around the presence of the risen Christ. The church is not the arbiter of its content but must, in response to Jesus Christ's own self-utterance to the church, *witness* to that reality of divine presence in its midst. We are a *hearing* (called) church before we are a speaking church. The history of the church—all Christians through history—is a history of the activity of the Holy Spirit in reconciling and guiding the world to God. This functions to decenter theological history from an account of human processes. The center is the providential activity of God in the history of the Christian community. It also points to how Christians should use the Bible.

When we use the Bible we witness to the One who speaks in it. Through the Bible, God moves our lips; we do not use it to speak *for*

God. We assent to the *viva vox Jesu Christi* (living voice of Jesus Christ), which is an act of confession and submission. In our use of the Bible, authority is proportionate to obedience. Faithful reading then is response as an act of submission *(mortification sui)*. This means that the church has much to do before it engages in its missionary tasks and proclamation, not the least of which is to be humble and silent in order to hear.

But are there any other texts God uses?

The canon of Scripture. In the early 1990s I spent a summer in the former Soviet Union and worked with a small Baptist church that had suffered terribly during the communist years and had endured decades of isolation from other Christian churches. The church had one incomplete Bible for the entire congregation. To complicate matters, one of the leaders, Pavel (Paul), had found a banned copy of *The Prophecies* by the so-called prophet Nostradamus (1503-1566). Because the language of Nostradamus seemed biblical, Pavel thought that it might actually be part of the Christian Bible, some part they had lost or missed. He told me that he often preached from Nostradamus and asked whether I had more Scriptures like it. Pavel was asking a profound theological question, one raised periodically in the Christian West when an ancient text from the biblical period is found. Is our Bible complete? Are other texts Scripture? What if scholars found a previously unknown letter by the apostle Paul; should it too be regarded as Scripture?

These questions are very important. How did the early church discover (or rather have imposed on it) which books are apostolic and therefore authoritative—that is, canonical—in the life of the community? The term *canon* reflects the consensus of the Christian community about which texts are normative for Christian life and theology. Regarding this, there are differences between the Roman Catholics (and Eastern Orthodoxy) and the Protestants.

Protestants have generally understood the canon to be tied to the notion of *praxis* or *use:* that which is Scripture finds approval in meaning and interpretation within an organic worshiping and confessing community—both past and present. This means (1) canon is largely measured against a community already committed to using and respecting the texts in worship and common confession; canon follows an *organic* development, meant not to exclude or restrict but rather to be a positive formulation of what already exists within the church and its practices; and (2) canon precedes the church. Even more strongly, what defines the true church is the location of a community that confesses what the canon witnesses. This is very close to what Luther and Calvin considered a mark of the church, being in the possession of and being possessed by the Scriptures.

There are some real problems with this understanding of canon. Perhaps the most dangerous is that it opens the door for discarding some Scriptural texts because they don't suit the theology or worldview of the congregation or culture. If the community makes something canonical, then God takes the passenger seat in terms of canon. In simple terms, a church can decide what is good for it, that is, which books, paragraphs, sentences work for its spirituality.

Orthodoxy and Roman Catholicism understand canon as the *imposition* of the church's authority upon the Bible. The church, in its teaching and offices, especially the leadership offices *(episkopē)*, comes before and decides what is canonical. Accordingly, God granted to various church leaders special wisdom or gifts to discern what is canonical. The church concretely precedes or determines canon, usually in the context of preventing heresy. Today the church is the guardian of the canon.

The chief problem with this view is that a few spiritually active and gifted *men* decided what made the grade as Scripture. If we fast forward to our present context, we can see that this idea is extended in the practice of men, operating in those same offices, determining the *meaning*, or interpretation, of canon. But the question then becomes whether God is shackled from speaking in a new manner. For the Orthodox and Catholic traditions, it is not so much whether some text should be added to or eliminated from the canon (for that is already settled), but whether some new meaning can be given to the canon itself apart from traditional understandings. For example, one of the criticisms that Latin American Catholics direct to the papacy is that the situation of the economically exploited is neglected in Catholic biblical interpretation. Latin American Christians want to hear the good news about God's love for the poor.

The dialectic between canon forming the church and the church as its guardian is a theological point of dispute in Protestant and Orthodox/Catholic churches. In both cases, however, canon cannot dictate textual meaning—it is only a measurement or rule of faith. Canon is not an ecclesial adjective; that is, something merely *made* useful by the community of faith and *its* acceptance of a series of texts. Nor is it merely the result of a series of historical accidents or special gifts to some leaders at key times. Rather, it is the response of the church to the present action of its Lord. Canon is an account of the self-communicative presence of the triune God through creaturely forms (means of grace) that are annexed and sanctified by God and, as a result, acknowledged and witnessed to by the church. It is, in short, the rule of faith from which the church acknowledges the work of God in the church—including the history of the canon itself. Canon is a dynamic reality of God.

Pavel's question is answered by canon—early in Christian history the faithful Christian community under the guidance of its Lord and the present Spirit gathered a group of texts, out of the myriad of texts in circulation, that best represented their understanding, and by extension that of all Christians, of the witness of the first Christians to Jesus Christ and the witness of Israel to its Lord. Canon does not merely mean to read as the early church would have read, but to acknowledge God's graciousness in using these same texts as vehicles of grace now. True, there may have been many other texts that may have fit the criteria, but it is God's yes in the Bible that is sufficient for Christian life, witness and worship. God worked in the past *episkopē* and does so now in this community, promising to be present (how dangerous is that!) in the reading and hearing of these texts in the freedom of God. This, of course, can also mean that God chooses to be silent. There is nothing magical about the canon of Scripture. The miracle of God is their very existence despite human folly, manipulation and best intentions. Canon is a subsistent idea in our theology of Scripture.

The canon is *closed* and *open* to the freedom of God. It is closed in that these books are sufficient, but open in that God overcomes mere words for the prospering of God's people and creation itself. It is closed in that we need to hear from other Christians, sharing in the same unity of Spirit, what those words have meant, but it is open in that we are also under the Spirit ourselves for a new work of God. That is the exercise of preaching.

PREACHING AND THE BIBLE

One danger with Scripture (and the sacraments) is that we too easily confuse God's freedom and gracious action in these material things with the actual materials themselves. To escape this reification or fetishism in the church, we must remember that theology does not proceed "from below" but is primarily "from above." In other words, theology as God-talk including preaching is the promise of God pledged in the work of reconciliation by Jesus Christ. Our subject of contemplation is God. To ask why we believe when we believe what we believe is to acknowledge *who* we believe. Belief and action are the externality of the promises of God and the presupposed presence of the Spirit. As a result, when one preaches—tries to witness to that presupposition—the preacher is called to a prophetic office. But the preacher's words are given direction by adherence to tradition, Scripture and authority. God is speaking in and through them. In a very real sense, preaching is *Deus loquitur* (God speaking).

Preaching cannot be a proof of the truth of God because it is a witness to God's coming, and no one can presume to control God's grace. God comes, but God never comes at the beck, call or whim of a creature. Preaching is not a bridge to the reality of God. We do not explain God or how to get to God; we witness God's coming. Certainly, God is interested in character, action and ethics, but let's recall that it is the job of the Spirit to make us pneumatic humans (Christlike) and not our job.

We must, therefore, speak *from* Scripture, not about it. So the preacher is a herald who is a witness to God's graciousness, rather than a herald of human sin or even a producer of action points. Preaching is sacramental—a sign *(signum)* of what is promised and received in faith. It is the extension of our baptism (electing us) and the Lord's Supper (sustaining us)—that God is freely and graciously present to those called. Preaching then serves the church by reminding it of the "That" of the sacraments and the "What" of the Scripture: both recall that "humanity [is] gathered around the one event."[3] Scripture is the "foundation of witnesses with an extraordinary call";[4] it is, in other words, the words of those who point to Christ. Therefore preaching, as Barth reminds us, is to "repeat the testimony by which the Church is constituted."

The preceding discussion has two profound implications when it comes to preaching. First, there has to be absolute confidence in Scripture as God speaking to us through the Spirit (which will moot much of what ministry students are taught) so that both hearer and preacher expect to hear from the Word of God. Second, we cannot preach without praying, which decenters the person in favor of God's person. Remember "yet not *my* will, but *yours* be done" (Lk 22:42, italics added). Once more Karl Barth, who for years preached sermons at a local jail near his Swiss home, helps us with a profound thought:

> Preaching is the attempt enjoined upon the Church to serve God's own Word [in Christ], through one *who is called* thereto, by expounding a biblical text in human words and making it relevant to contemporaries *in intimation* of what they have to hear from God himself.[5]

---

[3]Karl Barth, *Homiletics,* trans. Geoffrey W. Bromiley and Donald E. Daniels (Louisville, Ky.: Westminster John Knox Press, 1991), p. 62. For further explanation see Darren C. Marks, "'Over learned preacher—You Are Mad!': Nietzsche, Barth on the Advantage and Disadvantage of History for Preaching," *Homiletic* 30, no. 1 (2005): 1-15.

[4]Barth, *Homiletics,* p. 61.

[5]Ibid., p. 44. Emphasis mine.

Barth hits on the two points discussed. Preaching is referring to what God has "made holy" in the Scripture, and, as such, both the preacher, when called and prepared by being misplaced in prayer, and the hearer anticipate God's coming. Preaching is more than technique, relevance or learnedness; instead, preaching is (1) anticipation that God will come, and (2) praise that God did and does come. In older parlance, preaching is a spiritual *habitus*—a mode of praise and worship. Preaching is not only the speaker but also the congregation in mutual adoration of their Lord.

MAKING CHRIST PRESENT: THE SACRAMENTS

Perhaps there is not a subject that causes more confusion and argument in Christianity than the number, kind, nature and administration of (as well as the mode of Christ's presence in) the sacraments. Christian theological history is littered with disputes ranging from a description of whether Christ is *really* present or merely *symbolically* present, to who can give and receive the sacraments, let alone what exactly constitutes a sacrament. However, what cannot be disputed is that the church has always had at least two sacraments and that the earliest accounts of them, both biblically and in the church fathers, attach tremendous importance to them. The two sacraments that seem to be universally agreed on are the sacrament of baptism (although it is unclear in the biblical accounts as to whether it is adult or infant baptism) and the Lord's Supper (more formally known as the Eucharist or Great Thanksgiving). Our discussion will focus primarily on these two universally practiced sacraments. Like the Bible, the sacraments are everyday things and actions through which God's graciousness transforms or sanctifies persons in order that each may fulfill their spiritual destiny as God's creatures. In short, they enable the witness of the church to the work of God and therefore are an essential aspect of Christian life.

A definition. The word *sacrament* comes from the Latin *sacramentum*, which was used to translate the Greek work *mystērion*. Understanding the origin of the word is important because it highlights two aspects in tension. The Greek word, meaning "mystery," is used in the Bible (see Col 2:2; 1 Tim 3:16) and Christian literature to indicate not a secret knowledge or the unexplained, but the reality of God present in Christ and therefore known to believers. The Latin choice then of *sacramentum* is not surprising. The direct translation of *mystērion* (in the hidden sense) would be the Latin words *mysterium* or *arcanum*. The earliest Christians instead chose *sacramentum*, which was a solemn promise to be kept by an oath-taker. If we combine the two ideas of mystery and promise, we get a good definition of a sacrament—a *promise* of *presence* guaranteed by God. A sacrament then is twofold: (1) a way in which spiritual reality—Christ—is given visible form, and (2) a way in which God, as in the incarnation itself (the first sacrament), manifests the will of God, which is salvation (participation by humanity with and in God).

The number of sacraments has varied in Christian history. Most start with the two dominical (Christ-initiated) sacraments of baptism (Mt 28:19) and the Eucharist (e.g., Mk 14:22-26). Roman Catholics and Orthodox Christians list five additional sacraments: confirmation (*charismation* or receiving the Spirit, which allows a child who has come of age to receive the Eucharist); marriage; holy orders (ordination of deacons, priests and bishops); penance (confession); and anointing (unction, usually near death). (There were as many as thirteen in the medieval period.) Orthodox Christians, however, have an expanded list of sacraments. The Orthodox tradition holds that the entire world is in the process of being transformed by the presence of God in Christ, and thus, in a very real way, anything can be the location of God's transformation and promise. As such, images or icons are given a quasi-sacramental existence in the Orthodox tradition, the idea being that the icon is a mirror or entrance into the reality of God. To gaze on an icon is to be lifted into that heavenly presence. Thus the icons covering the walls and ceiling of the church are really the heavenly saints joining the terrestrial saints in worship.

Classically, a sacrament is "a visible form of invisible grace" (Augustine) and has the following four characteristics as defined by Hugh of St. Victor (1078-1141).

- A sacrament must have a visible or material element. This means it must be an object.

- A sacrament must have a likeness to what is signified. This means, for example, that because baptism is a washing of sin, it uses water. Likewise, wine looks like blood.

- A sacrament must have authorization or authority to signify—for most of the Christian tradition this means that either it is initiated by Christ or found in the Bible, but in some traditions this can also mean that it was found in early church practices.

- A sacrament must be efficacious. Namely, it must do what it is supposed to do.

However, there are some real problems with Hugh's definitions. The most obvious is that the sacraments of penance and confession don't fit all the requirements. For example, there is no material object in the act of confession. Luther used this exact line of argument in his final rejection of penance. He rejected it in favor of the more clear and dominical sacraments of the Lord's Supper and baptism. And the likeness criterion causes problems, particularly in a missionary context. Consider a society that is not agriculturally based, such as many aboriginal cultures. In such cases, it is not likely that they have vineyards and wine. Therefore another drink must be used. Thus many Christian traditions have changed the traditional element to one that makes sense in their context, much to the chagrin of many traditionalists.

Finally, is it possible that a sacrament could be surpassed? When Paul says that circumcision is no longer required to express faith in God (Acts 15; cf. Gal 5:6), he is really arguing, contrary to Peter, that a sacrament has been found wanting or has been surpassed. Could the same be said today about other sacraments? It all hinges on the subtle but important difference between *sacramentology* (theology of the specific sacraments found in the Christian tradition) and *sacramentality*, which is important among postmoderns in the West as well as in the Global South and its missionary context.

Sacramentality. Sacramentality conveys the idea that much, if not all, of the material world has some sort of connection to the Spirit and therefore can be studied as a theological manifestation of God. This assumes that the spiritual is *not* limited to the traditional loci of Christian interpretation but, in the words of Anglican Bishop Geoffrey Rowell, that there is "a symbolic universe, a universe which has the cross imprinted on it, the cosmic cross of which Justin Martyr spoke when he made reference to Plato saying in the *Timaeus* that the *Logos* was set like a *Tau* in the heavens."[6] Sacramentality is ecumenical, interfaith and expansive in its possibilities of the manifestations of the Spirit to tell creation and humans of God. It pivots on some arguments regarding the use of icons in the Orthodox Church first made by John of Damascus (c. 646-749) during the iconoclastic controversies of 730-842.

To answer those who wished to destroy the icons as being idolatrous, a theme repeated in the Protestant Reformation, John of Damascus argued one major point and several lesser points which justified the use of icons. His major point is quite simple: when God became flesh in the incarnation, this event announced that material things are not, by definition, antithetical to Spirit. Material things are justified by the incarnation. But John of Damascus was also careful to stress that in or by themselves material things were not Spirit. Rather, if God wishes, they could be places of divine activity (grace) so that in a sense they are replete with divine energy and grace. All he was arguing was the point that God did and can use everyday matter for God's purposes. So, he thought, why limit what could be used? Icons, he felt, were things used by God for God's purposes—though not in themselves divine, they are bearers of God's divine energy and grace, and become portals of heaven. Understood in this way, Orthodox Christians are not idolaters.

---

[6]Geoffrey Rowell, "The Significance of Sacramentality," in *The Gestures of God: Explorations in Sacramentality*, ed. Geoffrey Rowell and Christine Hall (New York: Continuum, 2004), p. 3.

John of Damascus argued that although God spoke clearly in the incarnation and has *primarily* chosen the Bible and the traditional sacraments as means of grace, these need not limit God's choice of revelation. Other things could be places from which God chooses to reveal grace toward creation and humankind. This is especially important in a missiological context, in which missionaries assume that God has indeed preceded the gospel in preparation for the reception of the good news of Christ. So we learn from John of Damascus that God is active and there is no place or person that is Godforsaken. Sacramentality also allows art, architecture and music to be locations of inspiration of the Spirit.

Thus, in some Christian traditions and in the understanding of some theologians, sacramentality is not a problem but is an essential declaration of God's activity in the world. This does not mean, though, that sacramentality is without problems. Some theologians, notably the controversial and censured Catholic Matthew Fox, have argued that sacramentality is a way of speaking of a *sōma pneumatikon*, a "World Soul" or cosmological "Christ principle." Here God and creation are indeed confused as to which is which. Fox thinks that everything, due to its own nature as created by God, is a place of Spirit, and therefore no one thing should be necessarily elevated as a better, fuller or more clear revelation of Spirit. If all is Spirit, then all is a sacrament.

In answering Fox, we turn to the iconoclast critics of John of Damascus. Their criticisms fall into two broad categories. The first questions the authority of the belief that God is present in everything because Spirit is not antithetical to matter. Can a new "sacrament" dramatically alter plainer revelations of God such as the Bible, the sacraments themselves and the church in its offices? What the iconoclast is asking is whether a new location of revelation can change what is more generally accepted as a sacrament. Can we simply discard what faithful Christians have passed to us because it doesn't fit our world anymore? What kind of criteria allows such a decision? While everything potentially is a sacrament, there are some sacraments promised to the church by God. These take priority. Indeed, for the iconoclast, there may have been sufficient justification for the icons, but they confuse the issue and create further theological difficulties.

The major difficulty does not question God's ability to reveal God in any one of an infinite number of ways, but rather is with the human propensity to make idols out of creatures (Rom 1:18-25). As our understanding of sin teaches us, humans are inveterate idolaters, and Christian history is littered with idolatrous use of the sacraments, from selling and wearing Eucharistic wafers as amulets to using holy water to fend off imaginary vampires! Humans have a tendency to confuse the sacred and the profane, and to want to use the profane to control God or at least God's power (see Simon the Sorcerer in Acts 8:9-24). The iconoclasts believed that the fewer and the clearer the signs of God, the better. Icons are not worshiped in Orthodox theology, but many in that tradition get confused and slip into idolatry. Iconoclasts therefore thought it would be better to remove all icons to avoid the possibility of idolatry.

What we need to understand is that despite a common assertion that God does indeed work in and through material objects, sacramentality and the sacraments (sacramentology) are two different things. Sacraments are special, not because of an internal property but because God has attached a special purpose to them and instructed the church to continue in them until the Lord returns.

Sacraments: An ecumenical proposal. We have a significant problem with the sacraments. If they are indeed so important, why are there so many controversies on their nature and number? The way forward is to understand what a sacrament really does, and looking across Christian history we can detect, in varying strengths, three aspects of a sacrament.

First, as Ambrose of Milan (c. 339-397) informs us, sacraments *convey* grace. This means that it is God's work in the material thing that is effective for the purposes of God. A sacrament is not a mere symbol (like McDonald's golden arches are a symbol) or a memorial of something past, but it is an object to which God attaches a promise of presence and therefore action. God's action is not mechanical or obligatory but rather flows from the consistent character of God revealed in Christ; namely, God elects to be a gracious and present God. Neither our faith, a minister's consecration nor our works make a sacrament effective. Only God's gracious presence makes that which is far near to God by sanctifying it and us.

Second, sacraments *strengthen* faith. This point is found most strongly in some Protestant circles and in Roman Catholicism following Vatican II (and in the fine work of Edward Schillebeeckx [1914-]). The sacraments bind us to *fiducia* (faithfulness), which enhances our trust in God. Sacraments thus both presuppose *and* nourish faith. To readily understand this, imagine that in receiving the sacrament, the hands of Christ give the element to you. In that case, we need faith to accept the gift as more than merely an object, and when we believe it to be from the Lord's hand, we encounter the Lord and come away strengthened in faith (see Peter and Jesus in Mt 14:22-32).

Third, sacraments are signs of *unity*. A sacrament is a token of God's unity, and therefore our joint communion in and with God is signified. This has been interpreted either horizontally (with each other) or vertically (with our celestial body and head). In the free church tradition, unity is viewed horizontally, so baptism and Communion are *public* signs of our pledge to remember our common origin and unity. In episcopal churches, this unity is expressed through the doctrine of monoepiscopacy (which we will look at in chapter seven) in which the bishop is the head of a body of believers, acting in the place of the true head of the church, representing that body of believers to other bishops acting in a similar role. The unity of the bishops, who perform the sacraments, represents the unity of the entire church because all the church is gathered in the common sacrament of the church itself.

The church is indeed *itself* a sacrament—a common place that fulfills the purposes of God, sanctified by God in order to witness the unity and vision of God for creation and all humankind. This, regardless of how the sacraments are interpreted, is an ecumenical statement.

The way forward in understanding the sacraments across traditions and through controversies is really quite simple—wherever God calls a people to God's self, God also provides ways, even working around human misapprehension and sin, to convey grace, strengthen faith and bind those people to one another, to other Christians and to the people of God. This is a dynamic of the Spirit, which makes a consistent sacramentology the goal in dialogue and communion but also opens sacramentality as an option for God, bringing salvation for God's people in different ways. This means that the church is itself a sacrament—a vehicle through which God is made manifest for the purposes of God.

The church as sacrament. Theologians argue that the church has long been understood as a sacrament. This covers a broad history from Paul (Rom 12:4-8; 1 Cor 10:16-17; Eph 3:2-12; 5; Col 1:24-28) through the church fathers (e.g., Cyprian of Carthage [d. 258] and Augustine of Hippo), the medieval period (e.g., Thomas Aquinas) and into the modern period (notably Henri de Lubac [1896-1991]). By stressing the mystery of God as active in the church, Christian theologians have avoided being both too narrow and too broad in their understanding of what the church is.

The church as sacrament has several important dimensions. First, the concept avoids juridical or visible reductions—limits on who comprises the true church—wherein the true church is easily identified with an office, person or place with all the correct rites and sacraments. Since the entire body of Christ, all Christians, is participating in the mystery of God and therefore the purposes of God, it makes it very difficult to determine which group, wing or tradition is the *only* location of God's graciousness. True, there are marks of the church—things which Christians must manifest or have, such as the Bible and sacraments—but these are boundary markers, which may even be clarified in communion with other Christians. The idea of the church as sacrament also stops the church from being defined too broadly as merely a human association. The church is not a group of likeminded people, however good they might be, but rather it is a place of divine action.

126

The church as sacrament argues that there is a difference in the church as church, that the church is somehow a mixture of grace present and human response. The church is not merely a human society, but is God's society. What does this mean?

- The church represents Christ; that is its mission, to make Christ manifest.

- The church in its sacramental role therefore is not merely about its own spiritual life but also represents the culmination of God's purposes for humanity and creation because it is the place of divine action. However, this universal mission is placed into individual cultures so that what is proper for the local is developed in the revelation of the universal will of God. That is, for example, churches in Africa look like *African* churches.

- The church then is the body of Christ not merely as metaphor or simile, but substantially and fully. In other words, church is the way God interacts with the world just as the Son of God became authentically human in the incarnation and is the authentic manner of God's relation to creation and the human creature. This means that the church must be active in the world, involved in justice, love, and peaceable activities and advocacy because its Lord is just, loving and peaceable.

SUMMING UP

How is Christ present? In the church. God initiates, sustains and brings the church to its proper destiny. How does this occurs? Through the Bible and the sacraments, which are where God's graciousness is attached to the church and therefore, by extension, to the world, so that all the world may know its Lord.

For many of us, this is difficult to hear. In the Christian West, our Protestant reluctance to answer this way needs to be examined. We live far more easily with our culture than we do with the Bible and the sacraments; that is, we look to culture to answer our "sacramentality" questions before asking our "sacramentology" questions. As such, we run ahead of God.

DISCUSSION QUESTIONS

1. In what ways is the Bible special or inspired for use by Christians?

2. Why is it important for Christians to think about means of grace or ways through which God becomes present in the community?

3. How are the sacraments and the Bible useful in the life of a Christian and the Christian community?

4. Why is the church important in a theology of the Bible or sacraments?

5. What is Christian preaching?

BIBLIOGRAPHY

Introductory

Cooke, Bernard. *Sacraments and Sacramentality*. New London, Conn.: Twenty-Third Publications, 1983. Roman Catholic

Braaten, Carl, and Robert Jenson, eds. *Marks of the Body of Christ*. Grand Rapids: Eerdmans, 1999. Lutheran.

Wright, N. T. *The Last Word*. San Francisco: HarperOne, 2005. Anglican.

Intermediate

Berkouwer, G. C. *The Sacraments*. Grand Rapids: Eerdmans, 1969. Reformed.

Rahner, Karl. *The Church and the Sacraments*. St. Louis: Herder, 1963. Roman Catholic.

Sauter, Gerhard. *Gateways to Dogmatics*. Grand Rapids: Eerdmans, 2003. Lutheran.

Schmemann, Alexander. *Sacraments and Orthodoxy*. St. Louis: Herder, 1965. Orthodox.

Webster, John. *Holy Scripture.* Cambridge: Cambridge University Press, 2003. Anglican.

White, James. *Sacraments as God's Self-Giving.* Nashville: Abingdon, 1983. Methodist.

Advanced

Osbourne, Kenan. *Christian Sacraments in a Postmodern World.* Mahwah, N.J.: Paulist, 1999. Roman Catholic.

Macquarrie, John. *A Guide to the Sacraments.* New York: Continuum, 1997. Anglican.

Radner, Ephraim. *Hope Among the Fragments.* Grand Rapids: Brazos, 2004. Evangelical Anglican.

Schillebeeckx, Edward. *Christ: The Encounter with God.* Lanham, Md.: Sheed and Ward, 1963. Roman Catholic.

6

THE DOCTRINE OF HEAVEN

"But in your hearts set apart Christ as Lord. Always be prepared to give an answer to everyone who asks you to give the reason for the hope that you have. But do this with gentleness and respect, keeping a clear conscience, so that those who speak maliciously against your good behavior in Christ may be ashamed of their slander. It is better, if it is God's will, to suffer for doing good than for doing evil. For Christ died for sins once for all, the righteous for the unrighteous, to bring you to God. He was put to death in the body but made alive by the Spirit."

1 PETER 3:15-18

THE VICTORY OF THE TRIUNE GOD IN CHRIST and the sending of the Spirit to the community of faith have indeed begun the kingdom of God, not only as a future reality but as a present reality as well. Christian hope in the last days, that time between the "tick" of Christ's incarnation and the "tock" of his coming in glory, is the time of the church and Spirit. Eschatology, the doctrine of last things, deals with the tick-tock of God's timing; as such, eschatology describes not merely our future—heaven—but also our present. The present is fueled with hope and the promise that indeed all things are under Christ. The Christian understanding of heaven, and eschatology in general, is a keystone in Christian mission, for it comprises not only our destination but also the journey itself, reminding Christians that nothing is Godforsaken and because of Christ's victory, heaven (or God's future) starts now for all of creation.

MISUNDERSTANDING HEAVEN: MAX WEBER'S CRITICAL VOICE

Money makes the world go round and loving it is the root of all kinds of evil (1 Tim 6:10). Over a century ago the German sociologist Max Weber (1864-1920) wrote *The Protestant Ethic and the Spirit of Capitalism* (1904), which drew attention to the relationship between Calvinism and capitalism, the dominant economic system of the West. Although Weber may overemphasize or misconstrue some aspects of the relationship between faith and economics, he does point out a rather important theological point: a person's heart is found where his or her treasure is (Mt 6:21). Weber argued that it was a *misunderstanding* of heaven that drove Calvinist Christians to hold capitalism as not only normative but part of God's plan. Although Weber could never have envisioned what the future would bring, his belief that this misunderstanding would result in a perversion of Christian ethics and the gospel was prescient. Weber recounts how Christian preoccupation with pleasing God and working to ensure heaven diminished efforts to be God's servant toward creation and other humans. Weber's misunderstanding of heaven, particularly with an otherworldly focus, breeds a misshapen Christian life and faith. Exclusively looking to heaven as a future event is a distortion of the Christian idea of heaven.

Weber argued that Calvinism's doctrine of election equated capitalism with election. A capitalist risks money in order to make more money, and Calvinists believed they could detect God's providential hand at work when such risk-taking was successful. This was evidence of a special relationship to God. Election in strict Calvinist terms entails that God from eternity chooses who is destined for salvation (and in some forms, for damnation). It is meant to emphasize grace but often causes Christians to be preoccupied with whether they are elected or not. Some Calvinists (but not all) used what is called the *syllogismus practicus* to alleviate this anxiety:

> All who are elected exhibit evidences of that election.
> I exhibit those evidences (peace, morality, etc).
> Therefore I am elect.

Weber saw a subtle alteration in the syllogism.

> All who are elected exhibit evidences of that election.
> I exhibit those evidences because I prosper.
> Therefore I am elect.

Calvinist capitalists, according to Weber, ascribed increasing wealth to be a form of divine blessing, a foretaste of heaven. And how we view heaven affects what we do *now* as Christian people.

Thus capitalism is, oddly enough, driven by otherworldly ethics. The Christian capitalist desires the fruit of the next world, which is manifested by financial prosperity. Capitalism's effect on God's creation or people doesn't ultimately matter. Election, Weber notes, removes the Calvinist from economic ethical considerations. Put crudely, what a person does *now*—investing in a factory that pollutes or pays insufficient wages—is irrelevant. Prosperity is the signpost of divine favor and election. Heaven is the focus, and the present is a mere stage along the way. Thus a capitalist could act with ethical impunity as long as it leads to financial success, which was evidence of God's favor. There is circularity to the process: taking financial risk leads to making money, which is a sign of being one of the elect. To see more evidence of election, more risk is taken, and soon the only real concern is profits. Everything else becomes secondary.

Weber argued that while thinking about heaven is important for Christians, it should not be seen as merely a final destination. Heaven is not only about the future but is also the present reality of the kingdom of God. Heaven is a Christian hope. But heaven appropriates all things under Christ, and therefore heaven is part of Christian responsibility *now*.

To underscore this point, let's return to Weber's argument on Calvinism and economics. Two important ideas related to Christian theological understanding of heaven arise from Weber's book. The first is that the present life is a holding pattern for eternity; eternity alone matters. The Christian capitalists' focus on the future reward of risk as a sign of divine blessing reduces ethical (and Christian) responsibility for financial actions. Capital risk, according to Weber, doesn't begin with the supposition that I must honor God by living by the gospel ethic (as the kingdom of God now) but rather with the goal of economic success, which demonstrates the blessing of God and my righteousness. But surely this is contrary to both the biblical witness and common sense.

Scripture is replete with those who suffered or died in their faithfulness to Christ and the gospel (e.g., Heb 11). The history of faithful Christian martyrs is well known. And our Lord was crucified! The world and the church do not have the same definition of success. The world is full of corporations who have abused workers and the environment, and yet remain financially successful. Are they blessed by God, or do they function as God's agents? Is it God's purpose that we all wear the same designer clothes, have a plasma TV and drive a Lexus, even at the expense of feeding our own families? No, the logical relationship between faithfulness and financial blessing is not at all a theological certainty. But those who seek the kingdom of God will know peace.

Weber helps us understand that heaven must not be an endpoint but must be a reality lived in confidence in this world. In short, heaven is a reality that binds Christians to live in the presence of God. This world is as important as the next one. This world is charged *now* with the expectation of the fulfillment of heaven, and Christians are called (commanded) to this reality *now*.

Second, Weber criticizes a Christian view of heaven that is entirely me-focused: what must *I* do in order to receive assurance that *I* will be saved? The Calvinist view that because we can never know our status before God, we must continually seek evidence inevitably leads to consumerism. Preoccupied with whether we are saved, we seek experience after experience (or financial success after financial success) to prove we are. The doctrine of election, which was meant to assure those in Christ of salvation regardless of their worth, works in the opposite manner. It forces a dependence on creating signs, new experiences, of God's blessing. In this consumerization of faith, the new and improved always supersedes the old and trusted. An individual's ethic is motivated by receiving rewards. In the race to be certain of salvation, he or she bypasses the call of the gospel to serve God and others, and instead tries to offset the anxiety about God through experience rather than the Word of God.

But what then is heaven if we are to avoid the kind of mistake that Weber pointed out? To answer this, we need to understand heaven, or eschatology, as the promise of God now.

HEAVEN: A BREVIARY

Eschatology comprises the Christian understanding of the last things, and has, at least in popular theology, principally focused on what happens in the final days of the earth (particularly in dispensationalism). However, for much of Christian history, eschatology is the fulfillment of the coming of God initiated in the incarnation and the final culmination of the will of the triune God. It is a theology of hope and not a prophecy of doom.

British theologian Alister McGrath reverses much of recent Christian thinking about heaven by making it central to eschatology and not relegating it to the end of the story of God. McGrath notes that eschatology entails several dominant themes that highlight a tension between the "now" and the "not yet." As citizens of heaven (Phil 3:20) living in the kingdom of humanity, Christians and the church are called to live in the now with the real promise of the not yet. We are pilgrims journeying to an endpoint sustained and promised by God, and regardless of the challenges of now we are comforted and shaped by the Spirit for theological existence. The biblical metaphors that illustrate the vocation and promise of heaven focus not on *my* projected salvation but rather on salvation as part of a community, a *redeemed* community in loving fellowship with its Lord. It is thus a future banquet, a city and a kingdom. We receive an invitation to be part of a relationship imaged in the Trinity and offered in the Spirit along with others who also live in God. But the banquet, city and kingdom already shapes Christian life, and this life is communally constructed in the church. That is, Christians are to live out their witnesses to the peace of God as a people of God. Two metaphors from the Bible are particularly helpful.

Heaven as the new Jerusalem. For the Hebrew faith, Jerusalem was both a promise and a reality, even when fully established as a real city in which the temple of God was located. As a promise, Jerusalem was located within the lands of the tribe of Benjamin and eventually became Israel's capital city and the location of the ark of promise and temple of God. Jerusalem would be the "city of peace" (Ps 122:6; see also Zech 9:9-11), the "furnace" of the Lord (Is 31:9) and the city of future (Zech 1–2). This is God's vision of Jerusalem, a place of peace, judgment and future for the people of God. It is, however, also a city of *failure*, a city in which human failure to live in the peace of God brought the judgment and punishment of God. Apart from God's intervention, Jerusalem would remain a city in ruins. But Jerusalem, as the prophets declared to the Hebrew people, would one day be God's dwelling place from which the Messiah would reign. Jerusalem is promise and reality, grace and folly, now and not yet.

Early Christians picked up these dialectical themes—promise-reality, grace-folly, now-not yet—which is best illustrated in the Revelation to John. In John's revelation the myriad Pauline and Gospel accounts of heaven are gathered in concord with the Hebrew themes on Jerusalem. John gives a description of heaven—the new Jerusalem (Rev 21)—as contrasted with earthly cities, including earthly Jerusalem. The new Jerusalem is a place without human suffering because all the enemies of God are defeated, including evil and death. Its walls and gates are guarded by angelic forces. It is a place of absolute security. And there are no more tears, no more longing for redemption or justice. Here all of humanity's hopes, not merely those of Christians, are fulfilled. The new Jerusalem is described as having walls, roads, citizens and even a "police force," because heaven is not an abstract place with clouds and harps; it is real.

Within the walls of the new Jerusalem are found the "tree of life," a "river of the water of life" and, most significantly, no veil or temple separating God from God's people. God's glory itself illuminates the city, and all nations, including kings, enter to give worship to the Lamb of God. Best of all, the people of God see the face of God, and God's name is inscribed on their foreheads, indicating they are owned by God. How magnificent a vision, seeing God's face (see Ex 3:6; 33:20) and living and worshiping with angels and people of all nations. God will dwell among the people of God.

Paul, John and Augustine of Hippo remind Christians that they are citizens of *that* city. By the present reality of this future hope, granted by the trustworthy work of Christ and the ongoing presence of the Spirit, Christians are called to enjoy the privileges of *that* citizenship. Today we think of citizenship in terms of patriotic fervor or kinship, but in the ancient world citizenship meant privilege or rights regardless of the individual citizen's worth. Thus citizenship in the new Jerusalem is a privilege, regardless of worth, due to the presence of the Spirit now (and future) and in which the church lives and shares with its surrounding culture the promise of the future. We are journeying toward this city, which is a promise made by the Promise Keeper (Heb 13:14) and gives us hope. The citizens of heaven live and witness in the church as the entire creation moves toward the culmination of God's history, to that coming reality.

The church then is called to a radical way of living—making the vision of John's new Jerusalem a reality now. This vision is not merely a dream but through the power of the Spirit is the reality the church is called to, what we are *becoming*. We, the citizens of and ambassadors for the new Jerusalem, live in the judgment of God that the enemies of God have been defeated on the cross. In light of this truth, Christians are to live in a different manner as a body, a community or a city.

The beatific vision. Another powerful image used to describe Christian hope is the beatific vision. In its classic form the beatific vision—seeing God directly—is given to Christians *after* death and eternally thereafter. The idea of the beatific vision is usually associated with Roman Catholicism, and the zenith of its theological exposition is found in the work of Thomas Aquinas (c. 1225-1274). It arises, however, from Scripture. Though no creature can actually see God's face (Ex 33:20), God's approval is literally a "turning of God's face toward" the approved, and God's disapproval is "hiding God's face from" the person (cf. 2 Kings 13:4; Is 1:12). Thus, to "see" God's face indicates receiving divine pleasure (or displeasure), and the beatific vision is partly understood as basking or resting in God's pleasure. The New Testament fills out our understanding of that vision when John and Paul speak of seeing God's face as a metaphor for being involved intimately and personally with God. To see God's face is to see God as God *really* is: love (see 1 Cor 13:12; 1 Jn 3:2). The beatific vision is seeing God as one who, in the Lamb of God, initiates and sustains love for humanity.

The Scripture's teaching on the beatific vision matures in the writings of Augustine of Hippo and Thomas Aquinas. Augustine tethers the beatific vision to Platonic philosophy. For Plato, the vision of God was problematic because of humanity's close association with matter. Humans, a mixture of spirit and matter, cannot clearly perceive the spiritual realm until they shed their bodies. But because they possess a spiritual nature, humans nonetheless are oriented to the vision of God as the highest good. Therefore it is possible, by learning to actualize this spiritual drive to God, to work toward the beatific vision in this life. Augustine and Aquinas agreed and disagreed with Plato.

The differences between the Platonic and Christian vision are quite simple: First, in Christianity there is no antithesis or inherent opposition between body and spirit, so the body does not have to be sloughed off as in Plato's philosophy. Second, the inherent desire for God found in Plato is in the Christian vision completely obscured by sin. Any movement toward God is due to the grace of God, which creates in the human heart a possibility of desiring God. The beatific vision, then, is a gift of the persistent grace of God and not an inherent capacity of humanity.

Nevertheless, Augustine and Aquinas agree with Plato that the highest understanding or fulfillment of humanity is found in the beatific vision. God is the pinnacle or endpoint of human existence. However, whereas for Plato the beatific vision comes from the *knowledge* of goodness, Christian theologians expand it to a relationship with embodied *goodness*, or God as God really is: Jesus Christ. Life with God is our proper destiny, which is won, sustained and nourished by God's graciousness toward humanity. As with Plato, this present life is to be shaped by the beatific vision, but unlike Plato, this is a relationship with a Being of love rather than an impersonal force or principle.

The idea of the beatific vision can become problematic at two places: (1) if it separates the body and spirit, and (2) if it depends on an inherent human attribute or desire for God. Both depart from the Christian tradition. For example, in medieval Roman Catholicism, the beatific vision was understood as the terminal point of existence, which raised questions about the status of the dead in Christ before and those alive at the second coming. Simply put, could a dead person, who has no body because the body is reunited with the soul in the final judgment, move closer to the vision of God? This, for example, is the vision of Dante Alighieri (c. 1265-1321) in his *Divine Comedy*.

On the other hand, when it is believed that an intrinsic human desire makes the beatific vision possible, it raises the possibility that the work of Christ is unnecessary. Christ may have died for sinners, but perhaps one great soul achieves the beatific vision without Christ or perhaps under the influence of Christ. In this case, Christ is not the universal Savior and Lord. He is instead an example or inspiration of a more general spiritual impulse that most if not all humans choose to mar or disfigure. In other words, humans have a natural impulse to God. This view, of course, lies outside traditional Christian belief.

Despite its difficulties, the beatific vision is an important way of thinking about heaven. It reminds Christians that what is described in the Bible and hoped for in the church—gazing on the face of God and knowing God fully in that supernatural vision—is the common privilege and reality of the people of God. As such, the beatific vision is experienced *now* in the Spirit-filled life of the community of faith: "Now we see but a poor reflection as in a mirror; then we shall see face to face. Now I know in part; then I shall know fully, even as I am fully known" (1 Cor 13:12).

THE PROBLEM OF HEAVEN

Given the centrality of heaven in Christian hope, it may be a surprise that for most of the last three hundred years or so, heaven fell out of favor in Christian theological reflection (except in terms of a morbid fascination with the end of the world). It, like the doctrine of the Trinity, however, has experienced a renaissance. At the turn of the twentieth century, Ernst Troeltsch (1865-1923) famously remarked "that the bureau of eschatology had been closed" for some time but was now working "overtime." Troeltsch noted that following a nearly omnipresent medieval and Reformation preoccupation with purgatory and speculation with who were saved, Protestant and Catholic theologians had relegated heaven, and considerations on the afterlife in general, to the appendix of theology as an epilogue to everything else that needed to be said. When heaven did appear, it was either as the antithesis to the much more interesting topic of hell or as a utopian dream—heaven on earth. It was then quite easy, particularly within the rationalism of modernity, to relegate heaven to a descriptor of some sort of ideal Platonic impulse. A hangover of the medieval world and its levels of heaven and hell, demons and angels seemed to belong to a superstitious world. The Protestant focus on the grace of God and appropriateness of heaven rather than hell tended to present them as the fulfillment or punishment of a moral self. Thus, for Immanuel Kant, the idea of heaven (and hell) was ludicrous in that it taught not morality as a duty in itself but rather encouraged a childish fear and shallow morality. Until the turn of the nineteenth century, heaven had very bad press indeed.

German theologian Gerhard Sauter (1935-), one of the best theologians of heaven, notes that heaven, and more specifically eschatology, has suffered during three distinct periods over the last centuries. The first period, by far the longest, runs from the beginning of modernity and ends at the beginning of the twentieth century. The understanding of eschatology during this period, the "theology of history," began to fail in the late 1890s. It was superseded by "consistent eschatology," which was replaced in the 1920s and 1930s by the "radical eschatology" initiated by Karl Barth and the crisis theologians. And like trains or buses, there is always another one coming. The 1960s saw the reintroduction of the "theology of history." Sauter reminds us that the importance of heaven and eschatology as a theological crucible must not be underestimated and thus can never be reduced to a mere appendix to the Christian story. Our vision of heaven comes as a result of other theological decisions.

A theology of history (c. 1750-1890). Given the European situation that birthed modernity, it is not at all hard to understand why eschatology was marginalized. Europe, following the Protestant Reformation, had been marked by centuries of church disputes, scandals, petty arguments and wars. Now infused by a spirit of hope as science, industry and culture emerged, and medieval patterns of thought were seen as superstitious, ignorant and harmful. Alfred Loisy (1857-1940) encapsulates this understanding: "Jesus announced the kingdom [of God] and it was the Church that came." Loisy's slogan highlights several themes in the theology of history. These are (1) the refusal to step beyond the boundaries of human experience in understanding God, (2) a view that the future is not determined except by human action, and (3) the conflation of action and idea (or hope) as the same thing. In other words, we make real by our activity what we hope for. How do we see this in Loisy's slogan? For Loisy, Christianity is essentially a message about God's kingdom as a grand social experiment which practices tolerance, brotherhood and a common origin for all of humanity. Jesus taught ethics and a positive view of human choices to enact his ethic, and the job of this newfound society of ethical humans was to create what Jesus thought to be the future—a peaceable city of God. Who creates the future? For Loisy it is not God (or the devil) but humans working toward a common vision. Our future is determined by our present progress. In the first century humans stood at the proverbial fork in the road in which Jesus summoned everyone to a higher ethical plateau. However, instead of following Jesus' message, we got a superstitious, hierarchical and ignorant church that complicated a simple message with all manner of theological gobbledygook. The future was dependent on human will to create good societies; it certainly had nothing to do with the church.

History is the slow and steady movement to this promising future, which is won by leaving behind the problems of Christian theology and in particular its view of heaven. Heaven on earth will be achieved by human hands.

A deeper theology of history: Hegel. Georg Wilhelm Friedrich Hegel (1770-1831) looms large in understanding how history became theologized. The previously unquestioned truth found in Scripture and the church was disputed, and the empirical sciences were steadily moving forward. Hegel shares the early modern obsession with finding a clear or undisputed point from which to argue ideas. Looking at history, Hegel came to believe that all the historian could do is mirror his or her own image, an admission that makes most of today's historians uneasy, but which is nonetheless profound. For Hegel, the observer of history is involved in the interpretation of its meaning, and therefore there is no vantage point from which to understand history. What if history is not a reflection of the past but a representation *(Vorstellung)* of something or someone that might reveal a secret destiny or development of that something or someone? History is a grand movement of an invisible

142

hand or Spirit to a destiny. Hegel clearly thinks this kind of representation of what he calls Spirit *(Geist)* is not uniform; overall it does move forward, but in the particulars there may be many retrogrades. It is the nature of Spirit that interests him. His chief question is, how do we recognize mundane history as Spirit?

Following the philosophy of Kant, Hegel argues that we can never see things as they truly are (as in the beatific vision). We only see a thing obliquely as it bubbles to the surface or is known by its lack or absence. What a thing really is (its essence) is not directly observed but only understood in part through other means. Thus, God is not seen directly, but is partially known through his actions in the world. Thus, to ask what is God like?—or the movement and culmination of God—is to ask what is history?

Recall that Kant believed that human beings share some essential categories of reason with God. God or God's purposes are equated with history, and history in turn is the story of human emancipation toward rationality and freedom of choice. Thus history is a story or the idea of human freedom, and it culminates in the freedoms of European republicanism. The everyday stuff of history—the desires of kings, the writings of famous people, the excesses of industry and so forth—work together to demonstrate that the only hope (what God wants for humans) is for ever-expanding rational freedom in all areas of human life. We reject tyrannical kings and leaders in the midst of their oppression because we want to be free or at least led by someone who is guided by rational principles. Everything then serves, for Kant, the "cunning of reason" or the "Spirit of reason," even great horrific human abuses, social incompatibility and evil itself.

Hegel agrees with this kind of reasoning but argues that Kant limits reality to mere appearances—that when one asks, What is this freedom? or Where is freedom? the answer flutters away to "no thing" and "no where." Kant's vision of Spirit falls away when we look very closely. Is this king, nation or idea really God? Kant must always answer no because for him true knowledge remains unknowable. It is always a dim reflection. It is everywhere and nowhere. It is merely an idea. This troubles Hegel because it never is real knowledge. Instead, Hegel thinks that while we can never absolutely know things as they truly are, we can, from evidence, come to a fairly certain confidence of what really is—Spirit. We can, for Hegel, know the Spirit by its effects in history. Kant's vision is a probable idea, whereas Hegel's vision leads to certain knowledge.

Why is this important? Remember that the quest of the day is mathematically consistent knowledge, unassailable knowledge, certain knowledge. Kant was great as a theorist, but theory is not fact. In contrast, Hegel believed his theology of history uncovers a fact—a true description of the nature of Spirit or justification of God's purposes. History is God's place of action, and an astute reader of history will not only see God accurately but also place history in light of God's future. One single point established on history's timeline demonstrates the logic of all other points and reveals God's purposes. In order to argue this point, Hegel makes some assumptions. First, he assumes that consciousness for humans and Spirit are one and the same. What Hegel means by *consciousness* is rather technical, but the gist is that what goes for humans also goes for God, so the realm of activity undertaken by human agents mirrors divine activity. This is critical, for it means that human actions, both positive and negative, reveal something of God and therefore of God's purposes. Humans are both subjects and objects, and when operating as agents in the world they not only interact with but also reflect something—Spirit, or more precisely, God's Spirit as human spirit. The something they reflect is indeed Kant's freedom, but rather than an idea, freedom is really part of what humans do. Consider what this means. A culture can be more enlightened by being freer in its values, and thus it more closely resembles Spirit. Likewise, a culture that is barbaric is also a reflection of Spirit by its lack of Spirit or freedom. In both cases, we see Spirit because of the spirit in us; that is, our spirit finds Spirit or its absence.

Hegel believed that though the series of historical events do not uniformly move from strength to strength, they do in fact move forward as a whole. This is simple to understand. Even a retrograde movement of freedom (say a terrible king or kingdom) creates the desire for more freedom of Spirit, so the next manifestation of Spirit (freedom) is that much more intense. The final point in Hegel is the keystone. The transcendence of God, the otherness of God, operates within creation and humans. Thus in a very real way "the kingdom of Spirit is created by human beings" because God is immanent in human spirituality. In a very real sense, humans create God's future because history is the crucible of Spirit.

A return to a theology of history: Two cousins. Two eschatologies arose in the late 1890s and early decades of the twentieth century in response to modernity and Hegel. The first is associated with liberal Protestantism and the second with American fundamentalism. Both share the following perspectives: (1) History has a purpose that is discernable through reason (liberalism) or proper biblical reading (fundamentalism). (2) Destiny is thus a divine framework and some historical events, cultures or epochs are of particular value as barometers of God's purpose. (3) Christian duty is to converge with God's plan, and our cooperation, our fulfilling our side of the bargain, is essential in deciding the course of events. This means that the individual's (or a society's or even a nation's) creative powers—choices—determine or reveal, in a very real sense, God's purposes. Let's see how two disparate movements converge on these points.

In liberal Protestantism, which is closer to Hegel than fundamentalism, the final purpose of God is Jesus' proclamation of the kingdom of God. Jesus, our brother, was primarily an example of piety or spirit, and he came to activate that similar piety in all of us. Thus the kingdom of God is the collective experience of our pieties. The nature of this kingdom is primarily ethical, proclaiming and acting with equality, tolerance and peaceableness. Thus Christianity, or at least Jesus, is the zenith of human culture.

With Kant and Albrecht Ritschl, liberals could admire Jesus as the human "Son of God," whose teachings most clearly speak of the essential and universal truths of humanity. Picking up from Hegel, they could even argue that Jesus is *the* central point in the immanent Spirit's timeline, and that the past centuries of religious confusion highlight, anticipate or yearn for a new mode of Spirit. Certainly *now* is the place of Spirit. Reading the Bible denuded of its supernatural superstitions, the liberals had a perfectly ethical, civilized Jesus and a new understanding of Christian history as well. They had an endpoint of history (the kingdom of God as our common destiny) and a few excellent examples (Jesus and their culture) from which to see the endpoint most clearly. The third point of the visionary trifecta would cap it off. The liberals felt we needed to work more deliberatively toward the kingdom. The church would become, in a very real sense, the great transformer of culture. State and church were seen as two facets of the same Spirit, and thus the flag and cross were closely allied. To be civilized is to be Christian, and to be Christian is to be civilized.

American fundamentalism, and particularly dispensationalism, also works as a theology of history, although with different tools. It too argues that history has a purpose: the second coming (parousia) of Jesus and culmination of history in the new Jerusalem. Furthermore, it argues that there are certain events or individuals critical to this unfolding drama of God. Clearly, Jesus is central, but the events—the restoration of Israel as a nation, the signs of the antichrist and so forth—leading to Christ's return are likewise important. The fundamentalist is constantly looking to history as proof of Christ. As in the liberal Protestant view, individuals are needed and even necessary in this divine drama in order for history to achieve its end. The creative power of the individual must not be underestimated, for it links fundamentalist dispensationalism to modernity's theology of history. Without the cooperation, usually explicit, of key individuals with the plan of God, God's purpose in history—the parousia—will be thwarted. This is critical in that it allows a reading of history similar to Hegel and Ritschl—namely that human spirit (creative agency) is the location of the Spirit. More simply, if humans do not cooperate, God will be frustrated. Thus the old adage "God holds his breath until humanity breathes" seems appropriate. It falls to humans to make Spirit work.

What is the problem with this theology? In *Paul's Letter to the Romans* (1922), Karl Barth made a significant point about the theology of history as it relates to eschatology. He notes that heaven is God's reality alone. Eschatology announces a new age won solely by God. Only God's certain victory won by Christ on the cross can inaugurate heaven as the place *of* God (the new Jerusalem) and *for* God's people (the beatific vision). It is new and coming because of one alone—God. Anything else compromises its certainty, and therefore Christians hope that in Christ God has overcome the enemies of God. Barth tells us that because heaven is the Christian hope, it is completely reliant on the One who is hope alone—Jesus Christ. This precludes the idea that humans cooperate with heaven's coming. It is *discontinuous* with human history. Barth's insight changes our attitude toward heaven.

Consistent eschatology (1890s-1920s). In 1892 Johannes Weiss (1863-1914) published *The Preaching of Jesus on the Kingdom of God*, which revealed that what Jesus taught about the kingdom of God was very different from what the Protestant liberals said. Weiss noted that Jesus and the early church believed that the second coming of Jesus, or the end of the world, was not only soon but also would close history. The parousia would call into being a new world discontinuous with the present world, and this meant that the theologies of history that assumed continuity and human cooperation with the kingdom of God had to be reconsidered. According to Weiss, Jesus proclaimed discontinuity between God and history, "this" world and the "next," so the liberal idea that the kingdom of God grows out of history through human deeds was a theological non sequitur. Jesus and his followers simply waited for God to act.

Albert Schweitzer (1875-1965) picked up on Weiss's work. He thought that the failure of the imminent coming of the kingdom of God shaped Jesus' death and the subsequent response of the church, whose complex theological apology altered the simple message of Jesus. Schweitzer argued that Jesus' confidence in the coming kingdom made him increasingly bold, forcing Roman and Jewish officials to engage him. And Jesus either expected to be delivered from death or in his death inaugurated the coming of the kingdom of God. The fact that God did not act in Jesus' death to end history reconfigured the apostles' thinking about Jesus, extending his return into the near future. But when the delay extended into years and decades, the church found it necessary to alter its theology. This allowed Paul to create, Schweitzer thought, for all intents and purposes, Christianity as we know it.

There are numerous problems with Schweitzer's assumption of difference between Jesus' and the church's understanding of the kingdom of God. What is important to us, though, is that Schweitzer made eschatology central to theological discourse—heaven and the "last things" do not belong in a theological appendix but are foundational to Christianity.

Schweitzer also noted that Jesus' teaching is foreign to us; that is, what he preached about God is very different from our desires and expectations. Though Jesus was human and not the Son of God in a metaphysical sense, he was not common. What is recorded of him is not easily digested by moderns. Jesus is a product of his own backward and violent age, and is offensive to the Spirit of our age. His understanding of the kingdom of God is unique. This provides us with an important clue to understanding eschatology—it is a revelation of God: God is breaking into, renewing and recreating creation in spite of human folly and without human contribution.

The problem with Schweitzer's eschatology is that Jesus' message of hope failed. Jesus sincerely believed that he was witnessing and possibly ushering in the kingdom of God. He believed this so strongly that he was willing to die for it. For us, the actual content of Jesus' vision of the kingdom of God is unimportant. That he acted on his vision is the key. We need to decode his vision—just as the earliest followers must have done—to make it fit our context and act upon it. Therefore, if we think the kingdom of God is largely an issue of social justice, then we work with the fervor of Jesus to help the poor and oppressed.

Thus in one move the old problem of history is reintroduced, and the "theology of history" rears its ugly head. The individual brings about the kingdom of God after all. So consistent eschatology, while initially highlighting the *difference* between Jesus' unique and surprising teaching on the kingdom of God and our natural expectations and desires, ended up with a theology of history. The difference needed to be accounted for and made sense of in *human* terms, and thus the movement, as Gerhard Sauter notes, "ushers us politely away from eschatology."[1] Schweitzer stops at the cross and adds nothing more. Jesus is a heroic man, a grand example of heroism and martyrdom. Jesus as the bearer of hope, or more precisely "the bearer of the hope rested in God," is lost.[2] We need not hope for what Jesus hoped, but we can hope for what is important for us.

Should we go with Schweitzer and opt for Christ the exemplar, using his death as a motivator to commit to a worthy cause? Or should we rest in the biblical witnesses and Christian confidence that God makes known the meaning of Jesus' death, as testified by his resurrection, his ascension and the presence of the Spirit in the church? According to Scripture, Jesus is *the* "bearer of hope" because the cross frustrates *human* expectations of the renewal of the world, and God instead declares *God's* renewal. On the cross, the witness to the *eschaton* (kingdom of God) becomes known as the *Eschatos* (Agent of that coming). Our hope is in the startling different, startling confounding Christ, not wishful thinking (cf. 1 Cor 15:16-19).

Radical eschatology (1920s-1930s). The theology of history and consistent eschatology did not produce a church or Christian civilization that could prevent the first global war and the rise of national socialism (Nazism). Thus theology was in crisis. "God in history," or God as identified with Europe, was dashed on the rocks of bloody battlefields,

---

[1]Gerhard Sauter, *What Dare We Hope? Reconsidering Eschatology* (Harrisburg, Va.: Trinity Press, 1999), p. 69.
[2]Ibid., p. 43.

and "God as hope" (consistent eschatology) was unthinkable as Europe was gripped by Nazism, the specter of the Holocaust and yet another global war. Europe suffered, and with the failures of the theology of history and consistent eschatology whatever hope God offered had to be absolutely different from what Christians thought it was. Into this situation arrived radical eschatology, inaugurated by Karl Barth's *Paul's Letter to the Romans*.

A few lines from Barth's commentary summarize the movement: "A Christianity that is not wholly and utterly and irreducibly eschatology has absolutely nothing to do with Christ. A spirit that is not at every moment in time new life from the dead is in any case not the Holy Spirit."[3] The first sentence addresses the problem with both the theology of history and consistent eschatology. In both, heaven is something humans actualize and therefore a function of human work. God might approve of what we are doing as a cosmic chief inspector, but otherwise God's not involved. Barth counters that because of the cross, the resurrection and the ascension of Jesus, the character of hope is "One Revelation"—Christ. Christ is not merely a metaphor for hope, the zenith of human development or piety, but rather is the in-breaking of God's true hope for humanity and creation. Hope is Christ. Likewise, Barth tells us something equally important.

In the second sentence, on the Spirit, Barth's point is that Jesus was dead, not feigning death or quasi-dead, but truly dead, and in that hopelessness God in the Spirit brought hope and life. Human hope is not the same as God's hope; human hope ends with death, but God's hope transcends death as the boundary of human hope. With the overcoming of death by Christ, made alive in the Spirit, human hope is surpassed, and humans wait for something else. That something is someone—the Spirit comes in death to give new life. In other words, God comes when human hope is exhausted; when there is no answer left, God offers hope. In its normative state humanity, Barth tells us,

---

[3]Quoted in ibid., p. 69.

lives in this advent of God, so human reality is faith, love and hope (1 Cor 13). Every point in time is a potential place of resurrection, "now" is "then," and true hope is in the One who is hope itself. Heaven is *now* because we are a people of hope, or more specifically a people in hope as continually being recreated in the Spirit.

Barth contributes two essential thoughts about heaven. First, God is always coming in hope to creation, even to the walking dead. God's future is not distant but always incoming, because the very thing that separated "now" and "then" in death, our boundary, is overcome by the cross, so the future comes, in the Spirit's gift, now. Our hope for God—heaven and the beatific vision—is the hope of God (Christ) made present through the gift of God (Spirit). Heaven is found now in our prayer and worship, whenever the Spirit comes. This is, of course, due to the very being of God, God's own history, which is trinitarian.

Second, we are not left pondering what God's future is, because the incarnation is exactly that identity and hope. The wrong questions, such as Who will be in heaven? often preoccupy us. Instead we must focus on the identity of the One who gives us hope. Thus the answer to Who will be in heaven? is Those *in* Christ. This limits the answer for Christians. Notice that no doctrine is invoked because salvation is solely the gracious gift of God. Our doctrines approximate hope but must never be understood as *the* hope. But the Spirit is God's freedom. God saves, and we know that Christ is the saving God and our hope. Nothing more is to be asked but is Christ your Lord? (1 Cor 12:3), for that confession is a gift of the Spirit.

Radical eschatology reminds theologians that God is free to be God but also that God is in Christ, and therefore God is known in that act of revelation. Through revelation we find (1) that human hope is limited because of sin and death, the enemies of God, but (2) that in the resurrection and ascension of Christ, God declares hope for the hopeless and a future in the present through the sending of the Spirit. Eschatology describes Jesus Christ the *Eschatos*, or the Coming One, who is already present in the church through the gift of the Spirit.

THE PROMISE OF HEAVEN

Radical eschatology seemed to answer many questions raised by the theology of history and consistent eschatology. But problems remained. The first and most significant problem is that Barth's Christocentric eschatology, that we should look only to the One who is hope, reopened the door to hope as an abstraction. Though Barth had a doctrine of the Spirit in his work, some (such as Rudolf Bultmann) extrapolated from Barth's Christocentrism that all we need is *faith itself* in God's rescue. The issue is that unless we consider how Christ is made present in the community and the individual, it is easy to confuse faith as promise with faith as self-generating expectation or openness to the future. Radical eschatology could be interpreted as existential philosophical theology. In light of their slender focus, radical theologians also found it necessary to reinterpret some classical themes in eschatology. The resurrection of the dead, the last judgment and the perfection of the world were pushed to the margins.

In response, a new generation of theologians looked to the Christian tradition to deepen the theology of hope. Most came to the conclusion that eschatology is relevant to daily life of the church. This needed to be addressed. Thus in the 1960s and 1970s theologians began to redress some imbalances in the radical program. Theologians such as Jürgen Moltmann, Wolfhart Pannenberg, Gerhard Sauter and Karl Rahner offered visions of a churchly, radical theology of hope, albeit with differing emphases.

A CHURCH OF HOPE

Having read the radical position well, Roman Catholic theologian Karl Rahner (1904-1984) wondered if we hope in the One who is coming, where do we find that hope fulfilled *now*? He refused the existentialist answer that we hope in ourselves as we take a "leap of faith," or its theological offspring that faith in the future is what matters. Instead, he argued that true hope must come from God. Faith, he reasoned against the existentialist, is not antithetical to the church, for the church exists to foster, nourish and witness to faith and faith's object, God. In other words, the church is related to faith, but this faith is different from mere belief in the future or one's actuality. Instead, faith, for Rahner, is *given* to the Christian and church as a fruit of the Spirit's presence in both. As a result, for Rahner, the history of the church, or the presence of the church in the world, must therefore be a part of eschatological accounting. For Rahner, eschatology is unfolded as the history of Christ and the graciousness of God, and the church, in its folly and obedience, is part of that history.

Rahner returned to the ancient Christian idea of the beatific vision. He believed that eschatology was thinking about a future now present in what he called the "Christological perfect." Following the radical school, Rahner agreed that Christ alone is the future of humanity and bridges the perfect and the imperfect, material and immaterial, sinless and sinful. Nothing humanity can do reaches that perfection in or by itself. The work of Christ opens a new path that is both the fulfillment and possibility of God's will as Christ declares and affects the true human, and declares the true God (cf. Heb 2–4). In Christ, the nature of human reality is judged, and in that judgment is both condemnation and re-creation—the end and the new both at once as God declares fallen creation and its powers defeated and offers a creative call to new being (new Jerusalem). All of this is the Christological perfect, the beatific vision as revealed in Christ.

Eschatology, with all of its intellectual furniture, then is a way of speaking of our surprise that we are recognized and subsequently recognize ourselves, our community and God in light of the Christological perfect. The beatific vision bleeds into the community of God by grace, and offers through its churchly practices real hope. Jürgen Moltmann (1926-) suggests this means that if eschatology is promise, then living out (or living in) the promise is the Christian community. Eschatology is not merely Christology (the charge against Barth) for Rahner and Moltmann, but also an account of justification and pneumatology, and because of those doctrines it is also an account of the church.

How do Christians live in the hope of Christ? For Christian traditions in the sacramental tradition, the answer is found in the Eucharist (Lord's Supper). The Eucharist is understood as the proclamation of the coming Christ, and indeed its biblical mandate reinforces this connection: "For whenever you eat this bread and drink this cup, you proclaim the Lord's death until he comes" (1 Cor 11:26; cf. Mk 14:22-25). In the sacramental tradition, participation in (taking) the Eucharist creates and sustains faith, and the mystical union between Christ and the human person is strengthened. A community, and the individuals therein, lives in hope as it participates in the mystery of the Eucharist (and other sacraments) and hears the Word of God.

For traditions with a less sacramental focus, sharing of the bread and cup is indicative of a community living exocentrically—that is, living outside its limits and incorporated in a body of believers that transcends space and time. In both cases the Eucharist is incorporation into the body of Christ, those people living in eschatological hope and expectation. The Eucharist is a foretaste of heavenly table fellowship, an extension of the coming new Jerusalem, in which social status, need and want are overcome. All are welcome, have their physical, emotional and social needs met, and exchange their sinful desires for God's reality. This then is the purpose of the Eucharist. It is the eschatologically distant future made real in one community-building event.

How does the church avoid making the Eucharist merely a human hope, a mere remembrance or dress rehearsal? Here, for the most part, sacramental traditions have an advantage over nonsacramental traditions. Sacramental traditions tether the sacraments to a theology of incarnation, the mystery of God's grace operating in the everyday and mundane. As such, the sacraments are means of grace—locations of the work of God in making Christ present in the Spirit—and as such the Spirit, in the sacraments, places us and our community *really* before God in order to live the promise of heaven now as Christ's witnesses. We are detached from ourselves and our folly in favor of a vision of God and the kingdom of God that is coming and declared in Christ. This is the highest reality, the highest good both *now* and *coming*. Nonsacramental churches can make a similar theological turn with a more substantial theology of community around the table as a foretaste of the heavenly feast. But often such a theology falls into an account of the surrounding social and cultural norms rather than an account of a theology of God's community. One has only to recall the role churches played in the resistance to the antislavery and civil rights movements of the last centuries as an example of such an aberration of a theology of God's community. The theological task remains for nonsacramental traditions to account for table fellowship as more than a human society.

How is the church (and its sacramental life) an eschatological community? Through a theology of hope. The church is the place of God's action in which, through the Spirit's gifts of Word and sacrament, the people of God are lifted into the promises and judgment of God so they are equipped to live in their culture, time and circumstances as Spirit-filled people. This answers some of Rahner's questions to Barth on the nature of the history of God in the church. The church is not some optional exercise or addendum to Christ's coming. Neither is it essential or causative. But in the freedom of God the church is allowed to participate in God's work, which is the miracle of God's overcoming folly and re-creation of all things in Christ. And the doctrines left largely untreated or marginalized in radical eschatology are placed back in their proper places. The church awaits the resurrection of the dead, stands in the judgment of God and will dwell in the perfection of heaven, which it already experiences in part.

A THEOLOGY OF HOPE

Eschatology is the amazement humans feel when they are allowed to have hope, or rather to know Hope. Humans construct all manner of objects on which hope is built. The Christian vision of hope is that nothing outside of God can guarantee our future; we find our true future, individually and corporately, in God alone. Eschatology is a theology of hope, and the hope of the church itself.

Why can we hope? We who were without God are now with God in Christ (Eph 2:12); we hope because eschatology is related to our justification. The hope within us was neither asked for nor deserved; it comes because God has a future and extends that future to the futureless. In Christ *we* were nailed to the cross, and God frees us from God's enemies and reorients us to justice and love by that judgment of the cross. We are no longer ourselves, but belong to the Coming One. Jesus Christ, the *Eschatos*, chose not to remain alone but submits everything, including himself, to God so that God and the Lamb of God will permeate the universe as in the new Jerusalem. We hope because the One who is hope comes, even when we contradict that coming. But that hope means we must also be sober-minded, watchful so that we do not confuse our hope with God's hope, become obsessed with details of Christ's coming or arrogant that we deserve our hope (Mt 24; Eph 5:1-11; 1 Thess 5:6; 1 Pet 1:13).

What is the reason for hope? We hope because God promises us hope in Christ and through the Spirit (2 Cor 1:21-22). This hope is Jesus Christ, in whom God acted in a promising way. God is the initiator who comes before and to us so that we can do God's will in and for the world. God says yes to our no. We can hope because in Jesus Christ God acts as a pledge of God's faithfulness and through Christ the Spirit is sent as a seal of redemption (Eph 4:30). God's history—the drama of salvation from Israel to Christ—is the reason for hope. God has a history and a future, and therefore promises our object of hope. Therefore individuals, the church and humanity have a history and a future of hope. However, this remains God's history alone, and all that is asked of the church is to be obedient to where God chooses to act. This requires humility, primarily as repentance, and the development of Christian habits such as prayer in order that each generation discovers its theological existence and task. What is demanded of the church is testimony in word and deed.

Dare we hope? All that stops us from not having hope is removed in the victory of God. Death, sin and the devil are disarmed, rendered toothless and judged for the folly that each attempts to foist upon humanity as truth, and for what each does to humans and creation. The church in its worship, proclaiming the Scripture and celebration of the sacraments is lifted into that dangerous attitude of hope and transformation. This is saying yes to God's already great amen. Eschatology is the content of our hope because it demands our attending to the task of hoping in a hopeless world.

ESCHATOLOGY AS A THEOLOGICAL MARKER

Because eschatology is the account of our hope, promise and mission, it is not meant to exclude, isolate and condemn. Jesus Christ is Lord of the church, but also Lord of *all things and places*. This is a different kind of authority than that which our culture argues is normative. It involves *that* articulation—Jesus Christ as Lord—as credo, in which faith is the freeing of humans to hear the Word of reconciliation God has spoken in Jesus Christ in such a way that we become for the first time and thereafter held fast in that promise of presence, love and guidance. How different this is from the modern version of the autonomous self, which assumes human construction to be absolute. God then is left to warrant our human cultures and norms. Rather, Christians are called to a different authority structure placed around the confession of divine grace and not of human power. The claim "Jesus is Lord" in turn creates and calls a community that also shares, transculturally and transtemporally, this gift of reconciliation and promise of God in Christ with each other and creation. The community's aim is to live solely in service to that freedom given in the promise of God.

What remains is not condemnation, apologetic or even persuading others of the truth of Christian claims. Instead, based on the confidence that in Christ God has become "God for humanity" and "humanity for God," that responsibility is located unconditionally and wholly on God. The church needs only to be church, living in Word and sacrament. It can do so with a certain cheerfulness (but not disregard), a confidence in God rather than method, apology or scheme.

Standing at the center of the relationship between heaven and this world as a foretaste is the question of *authority*. This deals with the ranking, essence and nature of the Christian claim that *all* things have been and will be placed under Christ's feet, so that no sphere of human activity will not witness to that *present* and *becoming* reality of God's redeeming activity (Eph 1:21-23), which the church is already proclaiming as real. In short, how do Christians reconcile the claim that God is active in the world *and* in the church without confusing Christianity or cultural institutions as the norm rather than God's claim on creation? How does the church interact with others without triumphalism, without becoming a theology of history or a dispensationalist augury of the future?

Christian confession demands that there is a purpose (telos) in history and that the *Eschatos* has ushered, is ushering and will usher in the *eschaton*. And though it commonly does, this confession need not become a theology of history, a history of the church or an analogy of being; instead, and properly, it is a description of the *history of One*, the history and identity of the *Eschatos*, who alone opens the promise of the future and quite radically and literally seizes the present with unhoped for hope in the midst of sin, despair and all manner of human folly. This miracle of *recreatio* is, I think, truly theological talk that always decenters human structures, always questions and interrogates us. In short, this is good theology or confessional theology.

Confession, or what I call theological theology, is the process of being brought under the authority of the gospel as church, and the church's learning to say *what must be said* from *what could be said*. The location of this formational exercise must be the church. Why? Only the church, warts and all, is claimed by its free Lord and his kingdom in order to enable that confession—credo. Divine action is confessed by the church, not invoked or confused with the church.

The Christian *obedience* to the kingdom of God is the confession or witness that God in Christ *is* redeeming all of human history and creation and, in the process of doing so, that God is also relativizing and overcoming all human structures. Christians need not fear that God is not present in their theological vision. Instead and independent of experience, they must hold fast to Christian hope that God is here; heaven is now. This is a witness to that hope that everything (including our faithfulness) needs to be brought to God's judgment, which is the word-act of God in Christ—a part of God's promise. Judgment then is a judgment of grace and persistent love in the midst of human folly; it is not our judgment on what is grace or love. It requires the church to listen, hear, repent and be Spirit-filled in action.

This is both opaque and hopeful. It is opaque in that it forces the church to limit its speech and action, and instead to begin *spiritual disciplines* of repentance, prayer, hearing and thinking (Christian habits)—putting the *theos* in theology. The church becomes a place of Christian habits. However, and crucially, it is hopeful because the church does not think of itself (or creation) as left alone but instead annexed or assumed by divine glory, despite human folly. The church takes seriously its role as a place under the authority of Jesus Christ and his kingdom.

Exercising authority in both the temporal and spiritual sphere is the same exercise for the church, namely, confession (faith) of (in) the activity of God in its midst as the One to whom all is owed and from whom flows all. This is basic Christian literacy or, to use an old term, catechism. This in turn is truly missionary, requiring the gospel's continual engagement with the other kingdom in whatever form it assumes—hostile, indifferent or sympathetic.

The church as a missionary presence in the world has at least a twofold effect. First, it desacralizes all human structures by placing the focus of any thick description of providence—God in action—squarely back on the response of the people of God (and creation) to its Lord. That is, Christians are not to name the world as righteous or sinful, but to name their obedience to God's promises in the world as they perform the gospel in that place. In theological language, providence is not a polity—secular or ecclesiastical—but the identity, via divine works, of the One who calls, identifies and equips the faithful for their mission of proclamation.

The church's authority lies only in its *witness* to the power of the age to come and not in any culture or an institution, including itself. Here I think of the Barmen Confession (1934) against Germany or Barth's letters during World War II as examples. In both cases theologians eschewed natural law conceptions of justice that equate polities—Allied and Axis—with right and wrong, and therefore God and Satan, and instead place theological judgments on Christians within those polities as being faithful to their called context. For some Christians that particular situation led to martyrdom, dying for peace in resistance to fascism; for others, it meant continued political and military resistance, with the goal of securing Christian peace and justice by tempering or resisting the sword. Both activities, however, reminded all of the lordship of Christ in order to prevent the church from becoming a shill for a polity.

At every point in its existence the church under authority must be engaging the other, secular kingdom by doing theological theology. It must represent its own literacy to its environment. What does this mean? In terms of the other (secular) kingdom, the church must champion its wider society, not parroting, withdrawing or simply criticizing, but seriously engage it. The church must always believe that any community, whether complimentary or antagonistic to its core mission, is never acephalous—that is, without reference to the will of God. If the church is a missionary church, it must consider how each human society and the church's own presence in *that* society is a refraction of the promise and reality of Christ's coming kingdom. This is remarkably fluid, but it means, in essence, that no political or intellectual community is ever deemed either Godforsaken or elevated to God's elect. To be truly political in engagement, the church must avoid the double mistake of confusing its own unique and particular narrative with a wider secular-based promise of salvation (even Western democracy), and also of never believing God is active in all creation. The church exercises what Gerhard Sauter calls an "eschatological rationality"—a dialogue with its surrounding culture that derives its grammar and syntax from revelation but nonetheless is real in its application and is open to the world. What the church raises is not merely a question of historical placement but how that historicity or "context of discovery" is pierced by the more profound theological "context of justification," namely, the intrusion of the philanthropic God into the human situation because of Christ. The church sees itself under authority and clings to its own theo-logic in order to speak clearly.[4]

If all of human history and culture is capable of being understood as the place of and transformed by God's intervention, the task of theology is to find, articulate and proclaim this intrusion of God. This theological task is completed in the practice of the people of God, who exist in the call, promise and hope of God. The church's difficult challenge is overcome by the difference of God therein. Dietrich Bonhoeffer is wonderfully helpful here as he argued that the church is the "hidden center" of creation, but only realizes that role when it divests its claim to that effect—when it realizes that hidden center as part of the freedom of God to be a God who surprises in grace. For Bonhoeffer, the hidden center is a community that is enabled to confess the promise of God won in Christ and realized by Christ, and is obedient to that presence; the church is under authority and therefore never usurps authority. This is what theological theology is—theology for the enabling of Christian proclamation, within and without the church, that Jesus is Lord. This theology allows for Christian representation: Christian talk, categories and identity within its texts and tradition. It is living in the new Jerusalem and in the beatific vision, discovering God's history as a people of God.

---

[4]See Sauter, *What Dare We Hope?* pp. 209-16.

DISCUSSION QUESTIONS

1. What is eschatology?

2. How is heaven important? What traps are there in misunderstanding it only as a future event for Christians?

3. Describe in your own words, how eschatology changed in the twentieth century. What are the strengths and weakness of each camp?

4. Why is eschatology related to the church? How is the church to exercise "eschatological rationality" in its mission?

BIBLIOGRAPHY

Introductory
Hellwig, Monika. *What Are They Saying About Death and Christian Hope?* New York: Paulist, 1978. Roman Catholic.

McGrath, Alister E. *A Brief History of Heaven.* Oxford: Blackwell, 2003. Evangelical Anglican.

Schwarz, Hans. *Eschatology.* Grand Rapids: Eerdmans, 2000. Lutheran.

Witherington, Ben, III. *Jesus, Paul and the End of the World.* Downers Grove, Ill.: InterVarsity Press, 1992. Methodist.

Intermediate
Moltmann, Jürgen. *The God of Hope.* New York: Harper, 1963. Reformed.

Ratzinger, Joseph. *Eschatology.* Washington, D.C.: Catholic University of America Press, 1989. Roman Catholic.

Sauter, Gerhard. *Eschatological Rationality.* Grand Rapids: Baker, 1996. Lutheran.

Walls, Jerry. *Heaven: The Logic of Eternal Joy.* New York: Oxford University Press, 2002. Methodist.

Advanced
Balthasar, Hans Urs von. *A Theology of History.* Ft. Collins, Colo.: Ignatius, 1994. Roman Catholic.

Bauckham, Richard, and Trevor A. Hart. *Hope Against Hope.* Grand

Rapids: Eerdmans, 1999. Ecumenical.

Bultmann, Rudolf. *History and Eschatology*. Edinburgh: T & T Clark, 1957. Lutheran.

Fiddes, Paul. *The Promised End*. Oxford: Blackwell, 2003. Baptist.

Lossky, Vladimar. *The Mystical Theology of the Eastern Church*. Crestwood, N.Y.: St. Vladimir's Seminary Press, 1997. Orthodox.

7

THE DOCTRINE OF
THE CHURCH

"Therefore, since through God's mercy we have this ministry, we do not lose heart. . . . On the contrary, by setting forth the truth plainly we commend ourselves to every man's conscience in the sight of God. . . . For we do not preach ourselves, but Jesus Christ as Lord, and ourselves as your servants for Jesus' sake. For God, who said, 'Let light shine out of darkness,' made his light shine in our hearts to give us the light of the knowledge of the glory of God in the face of Christ. But we have this treasure in jars of clay to show that this all-surpassing power is from God and not from us."

2 CORINTHIANS 4:1-2, 5-7

THE END (TELOS), AT LEAST ON THIS SIDE OF HEAVEN, is the church. The church, united in common vision and mission despite various familial identities, witnesses to its Lord, who is incarnated, sends the Spirit, gives the gifts of the Bible and sacraments, and ushers in the completion of God's purposes. Sometimes, to be frank, I wish the church was something more majestic and worthy of that gifting by God. But, nonetheless, here we are, given an infinite treasure to hold in our jars of clay.

What does it mean to be church? It means to be an apostolic, catholic and therefore *sanctified* (holy) people of God. It means to be invited to the banquet of God, in spite of our problems, for the purposes of God, which are reconciliation and peace.

THE PROBLEM OF THE CHURCH

Few institutions in Western culture and history are more maligned (often with good cause) than the church. It seems in no tradition, denomination or period has the church been spotless or selfless. Scandal, abuse, self-interest, open and hidden hatred toward others, and the like are threaded throughout the history of the church, and it is a wonder that anyone would choose to join such a movement. And yet it persists, despite its tremendous folly and sin, as the place in which God chooses to work in the world. The story of the church is a miracle itself and a testament that God comes, overcomes and works on God's terms alone. The church should not be at all, and yet by God's grace it still is.

For many it is not the scandal of the cross or Jesus that makes Christianity unattractive, but rather the many scandals of the church. In these scandals, the moral and theological problems of the church are highlighted. The *moral* problem is the persistent failure of the church to live in a manner befitting its Lord; it lacks integrity. The *theological* problem is the church's failure of unity, and in the popular mind the assumption that one Lord means one church tradition. While these problems are real and important, they are actually areas of strength for the church if it is faithful to its task and Lord. We should not expect a spotless or a one-size-fits-all church, because these would alter its message about the Lord. Let's explore this difficult concept.

The moral problem. Groucho Marx (1890-1977) is quoted as saying that he would never belong to a club that would have a person like himself as a member. His comment is a good place to start to think about the church. The church claims to represent God on earth and, depending on the tradition, may be a conduit for salvation through itself, its leadership (pope, bishops or clergy) or its rituals. Though God works in

166

the church, it has a terrible history, being intertwined with some of most grotesque events in human history. It has been hierarchical, oppressive and self-interested. Further, the church has had armies, owned slaves, persecuted dissenters and other religions, and accumulated tremendous wealth. Its leadership has adopted the dress, titles and authority of secular rulers, initiating a church-state relationship of mutual self-interest.

The moral problem of the church is expressed two ways: (1) it has been and often is as bad as its surrounding culture, and (2) it has been and often is too smug in condemnation of its surrounding culture. But what if the church is designed to bear a measure of brokenness in order to remind itself on whom it rests, why it exists, and what that message means for the broken, sinful and oppressed?

Some scholars associate the downfall of the church with its official recognition by Emperor Constantine (c. 272-337) and his famous Edict of Milan (313), which tolerated Christianity in the Roman Empire. The following years were anything but peaceable; while the Western churches enjoyed a respite from periodic persecutions, the empire itself suffered much in its continued decline. The apex was the fall of Rome in 410, when the Eternal City was besieged and occupied for the first time in eight hundred years. Nearly one hundred years of Christian influence, traditional Romans charged, had made the greatest civilization a ruin. The Christian era was in fact evil, and Christians, for all their vaunted moral superiority, were as bad as the worst pagans. This was the situation in which Augustine of Hippo wrote *The City of God*. In it he responded to the charge that Christians brought Rome down. His vision of the church, then, is a good place to start when considering the moral problem of the church.

The basic questions Augustine addressed were (1) whether the church should be very different from its surrounding context, and (2) if it was not different, was God then absent from it? But before we examine Augustine's answers, we must look to his own personal history.

Two particular controversies dominate Augustine's life and writings.

These are the Donatist and Pelagian controversies. The Donatist controversy involved what to do with Christian leaders (priests and bishops) who temporarily recanted their faith during a particularly nasty local persecution in Africa. The Donatist controversy plays out the more practical aspects of Augustine's theology of the church because it questions how the church should *differ* from its culture.

Also during Augustine's life, the Pelagian controversy arose, which centered on whether a person can cooperate with salvation. If so, that would imply that people are not totally sinful. Both relate to one's understanding of the nature of free will.

These controversies highlight Augustine's vision of the church as redeemed but sin prone, which corresponds to his understanding of the individual Christian. Both controversies inform us on the moral problem of the church—that it is a sinful *and* redeemed creature, but God's grace is able to operate in it despite its sin. In response to Groucho's comment: we wouldn't want to be a member of the church were the church left to itself, but it is not left alone. There is no practical reason to think the church as a *human* community will be so different from its cultural context, but as a *God-graced* community it can be different because it accepts a reality—the presence of sin and the subsequent need for God—that no other culture or community does. Thus Paul reminds us:

> God chose the foolish things of the world to shame the wise; God chose the weak things of the world to shame the strong. He chose the lowly things of this world and the despised things—and the things that are not—to nullify the things that are, so that no one may boast before him. . . . Therefore, as it is written: "Let him who boasts boast in the Lord." (1 Cor 1:27-29, 31)

The Pelagian controversy. The Pelagian controversy centered on the claim by Pelagius (c. 354-420/40) that it made no sense for God to ask for holiness unless it was possible for humans to fulfill that command. Thus, rather than being inherently sinful, humans, according to Pelagius, had to become sinners by deciding to act against God at some point. Humans had the choice to sin or not; they begin with free will, but the will becomes more prone to sin once it chooses to sin. Thus, Pelagius relegates two important Christian ideas. First, although he felt it near impossible (and certainly something that had not yet happened in history), Pelagius believed that it was possible for someone to not sin. Jesus Christ, after all, was sinless, and certainly he is an example to aspire toward for the rest of humanity. Questions regarding Jesus' uniqueness and deity are clearly raised in consequence. In a nutshell, someone could, in theory, be equal to Jesus in piety, rendering contingent Christ's incarnation and universal and radical forgiveness of sin. Second, Pelagius's logic of free will makes grace earnable. He argued that we make ourselves sinners and therefore we also ought to be able to make ourselves worthy of God. Put even more crassly, those who work to be better are more worthy of God's rewards and attentions. This was a grave problem for the church because it seems to make the church *worthy* of God, and what were "Christian times" in Rome but unworthy times?

To answer the theology of Pelagius, Augustine argued that without the aid of grace—revelation from without that both transforms the self's love(s) and informs actions—human nature, regardless of its education, discipline or will, is always prone to error and sin. The important point, however, is that Augustine applies what is true for the individual self to *both* general society and the church. Both secular society and the church are macrocosms of the individual's struggle with sin before God. This is hard for moderns to stomach because Augustine rejects our vision of the modern self's (and by extension society's) self-control and self-actualization. He envisions a self that is fractured. Just as people, both fallen and redeemed until the *eschaton*, are simultaneously good and evil, so are all human cultures. Therefore, in terms of the state or government (and the church on earth), Augustine expected a mixture of good and bad, right and wrong, and self-interest and selflessness. This comes with being fractured, separated from our origin in God. Our public lives are mirrors of our private lives. And we should expect this dual nature in both the secular realm and the church. We are vexed creatures, and nothing we touch is immune from our fallen natures. Left alone, Augustine thinks that there is little difference between any human institution and the church as a human manifestation. So, what is the difference between human society and the church?

To answer this question Augustine turned to the singular human. What's the difference between an unredeemed and a redeemed sinner? The Spirit of God resides in the redeemed sinner and provides the *opportunity* to unlearn the basic motivation of selfishness and to learn to love instead. Augustine asked, "What alters our *motives* in action?" He turned Pelagius on his head. Pelagius thought that what one desires is what one becomes worthy of obtaining. If I want to be good, I do good things. Augustine reversed this, arguing that what makes one worthy is what one is. If I am good, then I do good things. Was Augustine arguing that Christians are inherently good? No. He believed that Christians, due to grace, are free to love as God does, without selfishness. Because of this grace, Christian motives can align with God in the power of the Spirit.

Let's look at society in general. Augustine taught that what human society values is self-love *(cupiditas)* or self-interest through power and security. People make choices that benefit themselves and band together with those with similar interests. Sometimes, this selfishness produces good for others, and sometimes it is nakedly evil. Augustine's famous example is that the only difference between a pirate and an admiral is the size of their navies. The pirate works for his advantage; the admiral works for his and the state's advantage. Both want peace (e.g., eliminate enemies) and prosperity, and therefore work toward that end. The pirate may be evil, but his desire stems from the same place as the admiral's—to travel the best possible path toward his goals and to make life worthwhile.

Augustine then imagines a dangerous possibility. What if humans had a different source of motivation—a new Spirit that overcomes human folly and teaches them a different manner of understanding and relating to society? What if, rather than self-love, however nobly dressed, society was directed by a new motive?

This, of course, is the church under God, infused with and responsive to grace. Now the motivating factor or operative love—notice the motive is still love—is *grace (caritas)*. Grace, as revealed in the incarnation, is love for another (selflessness). Thus we have two places—two kingdoms—with different motivations organizing human actions. Instead of the self-love of the kingdom of humanity, Augustine believed that grace produces the kingdom of God, in which God's love *(agapē)* decenters self-love (however nobly disguised), seeks not power or security but to make peace for and prosper the unloved and different. This, according to Augustine, is exactly what God did in Christ in calling sinners.

Augustine's community, then, be it society or church, is the expression of each person in it, which has several implications. Original sin, being born sinful, means that humans, though naturally social, are at war. This war is the result of our "dis-order," being separated from God, which needs to be corrected from without, by God's grace alone. To overcome disorder, we need to be *converted*, and then by grace and in participation in the church as a means of grace, we begin to pursue a life of *caritas*, which uncenters the self's orientation toward sin. Christians seek to leave the kingdom of humanity in order to live in the kingdom of God (heaven). This means we need the church, because it is the primary, though not the only, place in which God works to correct our disorder. But like any human creation, the church is hampered in the short term by human desires *(libido dominandi)* and is in need of revelation in order to live in peace with itself and with its surrounding culture. The church strives to address human culture in such a way that the culture is shown God and given the hope of peace promised therein.

One more caveat: Augustine's theology is eschatologically charged. The church is a mixture of good and evil that awaits its promised fullness. The church is a place of promise—Christian hope—becoming evermore actualized. This has two important implications: First, until the fulfillment of the kingdom of God, the church has been both redeemed and unredeemed in its midst. And it falls to God alone to separate the two (Mt 25:31-32). It is not the church's job to decide who is worthy of God's grace; the church is merely to witness to that grace (Mt 20:1-16). Second, the church patiently remains in this dual state, and therefore is thrown by necessity into Christian habits to hear God's will through worship and prayer, and is dependent on God's coming in Word and sacrament. Finally, when it does come to church discipline, the church refers to those habits in order to allow God to pursue the offender's conscience *before* a local body decides to exclude a person from the community. This, of course, is a highly charged process across various Christian traditions,

Any church, for Augustine, then is an embassy between the two kingdoms and can identify some moral and cultural disorder, but can never cure the "kingdom of man" by itself. As such, for Augustine, the church is *missional* and not proprietary or arrogant. The church, while *hopefully* moving toward moral purity and living as God's people, is expected to fail at times because it is a mixture of saints and sinners. What makes the church different from its cultural context is grace found in the presence of the Spirit.

Augustine's dispute with Pelagius reveals that the church *should* be different because it has a different motivation, graced love. At the same time, though, the church is not the agent of God; it is merely a witness to God. The fact that it sometimes fails is further witness to that reality.

The Donatist controversy. The Donatist controversy provided a test case for Augustine's thinking on the church. During a period of persecution, some bishops capitulated to the demands of the persecuting authorities. The Donatists thought that those who were baptized or received Communion from a bishop (or priest) who had capitulated were not true Christians. This included more than a few and perhaps most Christians. In essence, the Donatists considered themselves to be pure Christians with pure bishops and priests purely administering the sacraments. Augustine's objection to this is simple. This makes the church, or its officials and rituals, as important as God's grace. Augustine felt this view was closer to Pelagianism than to the gospel. The Donatists argued that one had to make themselves worthy of God, whereas Augustine argued that God makes the sinner, even those who lapsed under persecution, worthy of grace.

However, after many years of trying to persuade the Donatists, Augustine made a startling about face in how he treated the Donatists. He asked the local governments to arrest the Donatists if they did not renounce their theology. Augustine, in essence, created the first Christian police force, or rather asked the state to do the church's dirty work. Augustine's reason for this action is central to understanding his notion of the purity of the church. Augustine claimed pastoral concerns for bringing the Donatist to heel by force. How could this be? Not only were the Donatists confusing and inducing fear by causing Christians to wonder about their salvation (bad enough), but they persisted in remaining *outside* the orthodox church and therefore were excluded from the means through which God might overcome their obstinate resistance. To bring them by force to the true church not only minimized their damage but also gave the Donatists the chance finally to hear God and correct their errant theology. Augustine advocated the use of force so that the Donatists might find God's voice in the sinful but graced church.

Before passing judgment on Augustine too quickly, it is helpful to realize that Augustine never advocated the forceful conversion of non-Christians. Only the opposition from within the "family" was dangerous to the true church. Not only did the Donatists think differently about purity (and therefore grace and the sacraments), but they introduced the most dangerous of Christian sins into the Christian community—schism.

Because the church has but one foundation, one source of its life, the possibility of disunity or having two (or more) churches was simply impossible. For Augustine the moral purity of the church is not essential, for the Donatists clearly had the advantage on this point; what is critical is that the church is more than a "pure" or "perfect society." This point needs to be pondered. Because the church is a mixture of sinful and justified, the moral deficiencies of the church are unfortunate but not unexpected. The Christian era, Augustine reminds us, is neither necessarily good (or even the most moral) nor evil; rather, it is the time of the church as a mystery of God's graciousness. In fact, a perfect society (the church) could become an idol, and would reduce the most essential reality of the Christian faith—God alone saves—to a function of a human society. The moral imperfection of the church means that it must preach that God alone saves.

Luther and Bonhoeffer. This idea of an imperfect/perfect moral church is found throughout Christian history. In the Reformation, Martin Luther, following Augustine, argued that the church is a macrocosm of the justification of the individual. Purity is not an attribute but a spiritual gift. That is, the church is the expression of the gospel event (created and sustained by God) rather than any specific human reality. The church too is a creation of the Word, and therefore doctrinal and moral purity are to be prayed for and anticipated in hope in the Spirit. Nevertheless, the church is a *hospital for the incurably sick.* As such, each church performs triage, bearing one another in love regardless of moral state and participating in the experience of salvation by serving others in love. Because each sinner knows he or she stands in grace alone, no one is rejected as being unredeemable. In fact, serving the unlovely is serving the gospel itself.

Dietrich Bonhoeffer picks up this idea in his theology when he writes of the "responsible human" and uses it as a way to explore a Christian community. Bonhoeffer wrote that while the church anticipates and prays for holiness, it is also always a community of sinners. Rather than being spotless, the church is called to be responsible and to cultivate responsible humans, which is similar to Augustine's idea that the church is the place of a different kind of motivation created by grace. For Bonhoeffer, a responsible human is a graced human, one who experiences God's grace and extends it to others, regardless of their moral worth (Lk 6:27-42).

Despite its sinful nature the church should not neglect its call to and anticipation of purity in the new life. Unfortunately liberal Protestantism often commends or accepts sin in a community of sinners, and therefore nothing further is prayed for or expected. Bonhoeffer reminds us that our confession of brokenness is not the only word heard in the church. For Bonhoeffer, being sinners is not the end of the story; rather the church is where our woundedness is overcome by God. In faithfulness we pray for and anticipate God's healing. Nor does Christian love mean mere inclusion, which can become an idol. The gospel calls us to new life. The church must strive in Christian habits to its destiny and vision of God given in the Spirit. This is transformative love.

As sinners, we know that we who were far are brought near, and we who are unlovely are loved because of God in Christ. That is the human story because it is God's story: "God *summons* them back to the origin so that they shall no longer be good and evil but justified and sanctified sinners."[1] The church is not a pure or perfect society, nor should it be. Though it has many problems, it is not left to itself, and its very weakness may in fact be its greatest strength—for who would see God in Christ if the church were Pelagian (morally capable) or Donatist (morally pure)?

> Here is a trustworthy saying that deserves full acceptance: Christ Jesus came into the world to save sinners—of whom I am the worst. But for that very reason I was shown mercy so that in me, the worst of sinners, Christ Jesus might display his unlimited patience as an example for those who would believe on him and receive eternal life. (1 Tim 1:15-16)

The theological problem. God's Word calls Christians to a unified core, voice or presence. But Christian history reveals a quite different

---

[1]Dietrich Bonhoeffer, *Ethics*, ed. Eberhard Bethge, trans. Neville Horton Smith (London: SCM, 1960), p. 182. Emphasis mine.

story: even the earliest biblical accounts are really about disunity. Disunity is the theological problem facing the church. If the church has but one source, why are there so many different churches? To answer this problem, we will start with the Nicene Creed, the first ecumenical statement on the nature of the church, and explore the meaning of one church, which is (to rephrase the Nicene Creed) apostolic, holy and therefore catholic.

Apostolic church. The church is a dynamic reality, an exchange between God and humanity, both redeemed and unredeemed. The church is an article of faith—we *believe*—and it is not accidental that in the Nicene Creed the church comes in the final article of a long series of statements about God, Christ and Spirit. The church is dependent on a series of more dominant theological truths: God the creator, the incarnation, the cross, the resurrection and the kingdom (eschatology). The church witnesses to the risen Lord Jesus Christ. The doctrine of the church speaks of the particular *history* between God and humanity between Christ's first and second comings. During this time God allows people to live as his friends. The friends of God witness to God's reconciliation to the world, which took place in Jesus Christ. God allows this community of people to be *heralds* and *ambassadors* of the victory of God, members in a new kingdom. This is the first definition—that the church is apostolic.

The apostolic church embraces the Nicene Creed: belief in the triune Father, Son and Holy Spirit, and the forgiveness of sins, life everlasting and the world to come. All churches that profess and live in these realities continue in the teaching of the apostles.

> They devoted themselves to the apostles' teaching and to the fellowship, to the breaking of bread and to prayer. Everyone was filled with awe, and many wonders and miraculous signs were done by the apostles. All the believers were together and had everything in common. Selling their possessions and goods, they gave to anyone as he had need. Every day they continued to meet together in the temple courts. They broke bread in their homes and ate together with glad and sin-

cere hearts, praising God and enjoying the favor of all the people. And the Lord added to their number daily those who were being saved. (Acts 2:42-47)

Holy church. The Nicene Creed starts with one *holy* church. To be holy is to be set aside by God for God's purposes. The church is where the holy God initiates relationship with humanity, so it is where humans enjoy communion with God and the promise of communion with other Christians. The church is separated *by* God *for* God in order to witness to that originating holiness. Karl Barth helpfully wrote that "the Church is a summons *(evocatio)*, a calling forth of God's people, the community of faith, which is created through Christ and the foundation of God's covenant with [Christ] for humanity and God, and in which the Spirit is awakened."[2]

We have to be careful not to confuse holiness with purity or moral superiority. This, we learned from the Donatist controversy, confuses the church with Christ. Instead, holiness is not an attribute of the church but a statement of its *use* by God for the purposes of God. Classically, theologians have called the holiness or glory of the church an "alien" holiness or glory. The church's holiness is a divine act of grace. The church and the sacraments make Christ available to us because Christ makes the church and sacraments available to himself. Therefore the church's holiness is not an attribute or state but more of a function, its apostolic witness, becoming real. Because it is holy, the church becomes what it is destined to be as it is obedient to its head, Christ. Put in a completely different way, when the church prayerfully and obediently anticipates, seeks and honors its Lord, it finds itself lifted into the dynamic nexus of God for *that* mission and *that* time. Holiness is a description of God and God's purposes, and not an attribute of a congregation.

One advantage of tethering the holiness of the church to its function is that it opens the definition of holiness more widely to include non-

---

[2]Karl Barth, "The Concept of the Church [1927]," in *Theology and Church: Shorter Writings 1920-1928*, trans. L. Pettibone Smith (New York: Harper and Row, 1962), p. 274.

sacramental churches. These are those churches in which the two primary sacraments—Communion and baptism—are used more as signs of communal fellowship than as a sign of fellowship with God. If holiness is defined as being used by God, then it is possible to understand holiness in terms of using the Bible and biblical preaching. This point makes many theologians nervous, as evidenced by Karl Rahner's insistence that sacraments must be accompanied by the office of bishop to give confidence to the Christian. But I believe when nonsacramental traditions persist in biblical preaching, they too are holy, since the Bible itself is a sacrament of God—namely, a way in which God calls people to God's self for the purposes of God, which is our sanctification or holiness. A holy church is therefore one that joins all churches in the mission of God's people, equipped by the presence of God in Word and sacrament.

Catholic church. The term *catholic* (universal) refers to the church everywhere and in every time as the place of witness to the originating holiness or call of God in Christ. To be catholic is to join in the transtemporal, transcultural and trans-spatial communion of all those who have engaged in witness to God as found in the apostolic church. Catholicity is thus a function of communion, and communion has been a primary motif in understanding the church over the last century.

Communion in the last century is largely an account of the fellowship of believers, both at the local level of a particular church and all other Christian churches that make up the universal church. The theology of communion has been greatly influenced by the work of John Zizoulas, a French Orthodox theologian whose work on the Trinity emphasized the friendship or fellowship within the Trinity. Because the Trinity, he argued, is essentially a relationship or fellowship, it follows that this same relational aspect should extend to that which God creates. Since the church is an icon of the Trinity and the pinnacle of God's purposes in creation, it must also be a communion itself. It must be catholic in its communion. Catholicity, communion itself, is an attribute of the Trinity and thus is an attribute of churches who share in the trinitarian purpose of fellowship.

The sacraments are central to Zizoulas's thought as the location of communion. In essence, he argues that the incarnation, as the central revelation of God, is the expression or foundation of all communion, and since the time of Christ the incarnation is *fully* found in eucharistic celebration. In short, Christ is truly and fully in the Eucharist. As each local community then celebrates the Lord's Supper, it also participates in the fullness of Christ and communion with God. Thus, wherever Christians participate in the Eucharist, they are in communion with each other. But there is one more wrinkle to consider. Since, for Orthodoxy, the bishop is the "icon of the Eucharistic *ecstasis*" (i.e., when the bishop administers the rite, the Holy Spirit comes), each bishop is also the representation of the fullness of his church. The bishop, as the Eucharist celebrant, embodies the fullness of communion between God and that people. But there is also another communion operative. Because each bishop represents the communion of God to a congregation, it follows that each bishop represents to other bishops that community, and thus the communion of bishops is a representation of the communion of each congregation. This idea is classically known as "monoepiscopacy"—one bishop and one church in one church of bishops. This is the primary way through which the churches have resolved controversies, through councils of bishops.

The strength of monoepiscopacy is that it provides a mechanism for churches to interact with other churches. This relationship helps clarify what is essential Christianity (i.e., ecumenical councils) and what is not. Perhaps even more important, but far more subtle, is the close connection between any given church and the requirement of the Spirit. One of Zizoulas's more penetrating insights is that many traditions have forgotten the relationship between Christology, church and Spirit. He argues that when the office of bishop is identified with the true church, the relationship between Christ and Spirit and therefore between church and Spirit was lost. His logic is quite simple. The church is pneumatically or spiritually constituted, and the church only knows Christ in the Spirit. But somewhere along the line, this dynamic relationship was severed for a more static model. The static model holds that the church *is* Christ's representative in a concrete fashion, and thus the church became monolithic and institutionalized. The result is that the church became top-heavy, and the laity, everyday people, is left out of the process of discerning the Spirit. Zizoulas's vision is startling: he argues for a dynamic Spirit-filled church—the Spirit's presence in the Eucharist—in which no one congregation should work in isolation to its gospel witness but instead is *obligated* to be in communion with other Christians, even outside its own denomination.

But Zizoulas's vision has several problems that need to be considered. Clearly, for Zizoulas the epicenter of the church is the bishop and the Eucharist. His vision of a laity-clergy communion is still rather top-heavy. But the Sobornost movement in Zizoulas's own Orthodox tradition attempts to redress this trajectory. This movement tries to overturn the overt clericalism and passivity of the laity by stressing that both the community and each member therein are unified and independent. It picks up the theme of "diversity in unity" by reintroducing the idea that since each *member* of the church has the Spirit (participates in the Eucharist), and where the Spirit is, there the church is, then it follows that all believers (and not just clergy or the episcopacy) are necessary for the church. In this case, the bishop holds his role in trust, as a steward, rather than as an automatic attribute of office. More problematic, however, is a common spinoff from Zizoulas that takes his principle that a local church is "persons-in-communion" while the universal church is "churches-in-communion" to its logical conclusion. In other words, as a local congregation gathers around the unity of the Eucharist, because of the presence of the sacramental action of God in bringing about unity in diversity, there is without exception communion. This means that communion is a *byproduct* of a local church's gathering.

This is problematic, and it misrepresents Zizoulas. Its understanding of embodiment is taken from phenomenological philosophy rather than theology. Phenomenology begins with the phenomena or experience of embodiment (having a body), which is both an object and subject. The body (individually or corporately) is an *object* for others to interact with and also a *subject* for ourselves through which we learn, in the process of interacting with other bodies, who we "really are." In other words, our bodies in interaction with other bodies tell us something about ourselves in a continual feedback loop. The more interaction, the more self-knowledge we have. There is in this account no real personal or corporate identity; identity is always growing, changing and adapting.

This phenomenological understanding is extended to the church as a spiritual body—in relating to other spiritual bodies, it becomes real. The theological problem here is nuanced but important. To answer the question Who is Christ? I simply need to look at the assembly of other Christians (not God, the Bible or sacraments). God becomes a function of what theologians call *Lebenspraxis*—life commitments or values of the community. If the community, for example, thinks (possibly with its culture) that freedom is important, then its God values freedom. If tolerance is a cultural norm, then God values tolerance. And so forth. What is left out is the possibility of God breaking the system open in a Spirit-filled manner via the Bible or sacraments. God's voice is excluded in the traditional Christian sense. The community determines the identity of the church. Christ's presence in Communion becomes what *we* make it to mean. A good theology, however, of the sacraments can address this propensity.

However problematic catholicity is as a general concept, it becomes more problematic when it is detached from the other descriptors in the Nicene Creed. The church's catholicity is due to its apostolic mission given warrant (and reality) by the sanctification of the people of God. The action of the Holy Spirit unites Christians to one another, through which they become partakers of the one bread and cup, and to one mission as heralds or witnesses in the communion of the Holy Spirit.

One church. A good definition of Christian unity—one church—is that an apostolic church manifests the communion commissioned by Jesus Christ for the purpose of proclaiming and manifesting his continued ministry using the gifts of God's presence in Word and sacrament. Unity is the sum total of holiness, catholicity and apostolicity. This nevertheless includes some tensions, which we will explore.

The first tension was raised by Karl Rahner. He asked whether we need an institutional church, with bishops, priests and so forth, in order to have the mission of the church. In other words, does unity come out of organization, or does organization arise from unity? Classically, this is the tension between *koinonia* (fellowship of believers) and *diakonia* (specialized service to that fellowship). Traditionally, and reinforced in recent papal pronouncements, the answer is that a highly specialized group is needed for the people of God to do mission or serve in the name of Christ. This is the foundation for specialized roles and offices, which enable and manage the mission. Thus, the role of bishops as the successors to the apostles is very important in Roman Catholicism and Orthodoxy. Roman Catholicism and Orthodoxy claim apostolic succession, which is an unbroken historical chain of consecrated bishops from the apostles (and Peter in particular) to the present.

In theory Peter (or another apostle in a different locale) laid hands on his successor, who in turn did likewise. Thus, there is and has always been a management structure that enables the church to the function and represents the unity of the church. This structure is the *diakonia* of the church, and it enables the *koinonia* in a church and between churches. Therefore *diakonia* establishes communion. For Protestant episcopal traditions, such as the Anglican and some Lutheran traditions, and for many free churches who have episcopal ranks, the opposite tack is taken. In these cases, the church organizes or makes manifest the need for offices to assist that function. Mission results in a people of God *(koinonia)* who in turn require organization *(diakonia)* to clarify that mission. Communion then establishes service in the offices.

For much of the world's Christians, the Protestant episcopal model is normative, not the older Roman Catholic and Orthodox models. In the Global South, Christianity is experiencing rapid growth and innovation, and therefore church leadership styles *(diakonia)* are constantly evolving out of the need to organize the growth of the churches *(koinonia)*. These largely local movements are aware of their own fullness of Church in church, and, like Zizoulas's comment on the relationship between Spirit and church, they are pneumatological or Spirit-filled. Thus the unity of the church is found in a symbiotic relationship of *diakonia* and *koinonia*. Both operate in a Spirit dynamic of Christian leadership models. One leads to the other and vice versa in the missiological context of global Christianity.

We need to return to our earlier considerations of how the church is holy, apostolic and catholic. My definitions did not explain how communion is achieved in office or how office breeds communion. I simply maintain that communion—the unity of the church—is a fruit of the Spirit. As Henri de Lubac says, "The Church *is* the completion of the movement of grace itself"[3] or of God's sum total work of revelation. Therefore, we can say with Cyprian of Carthage (d. 258) that "one cannot have God for Father who has not the Church for mother." Here I define the church as those called by the Spirit, equipped by the Spirit for the work of God in Christ, for the purposes of the triune God as declared in the coming of God in Christ:

Irenaeus (d. 202) wrote: "Having but one soul and a single heart, [the church] preaches, teaches and hands on this faith with a unanimous voice, as if possessing only one mouth." May we too be counted among those of that soul and heart.

DISCUSSION QUESTIONS

1. What do we learn about the nature of the church from Augustine's interaction with the Pelagians and Donatists?

---

[3]Henri de Lubac, *Catholicism: Christ and the Common Destiny of Man* (San Francisco: Ignatius Press, 1988), p. 58.

2. Why is the church's unity, apostolicity and holiness an article of faith?

3. What is the relationship of the sacraments and the Bible to the church?

4. Does the church need to be formally organized as envisioned by Roman Catholicism or Orthodoxy? What are the strengths and weaknesses of such formal organization?

5. What gives Christians communion with each other?

BIBLIOGRAPHY

Introductory

Braaten, Carl. *Mother Church*. Minneapolis: Fortress, 1999. Ecumenical Lutheran.

Congar, Yves. *The Mystery of the Church*. London: Chapman, 1960. Roman Catholic.

Dulles, Avery. *Models of the Church*. New York: Macmillan, 1976. Roman Catholic.

Kärkkäinen, Veli-Matti. *An Introduction to Ecclesiology*. Downers Grove, Ill.: InterVarsity Press, 2006. Ecumenical evangelical.

Schwarz, Hans. *The Church*. Philadelphia: Fortress, 1983. Lutheran.

Intermediate

Bulgakov, Sergius. *The Bride of the Lamb*. Edinburgh: T & T Clark, 2002. Orthodox.

Evans, Gillian. *The Church and Churches*. New York: Cambridge University Press, 1994. Ecumenical.

Clowney, Edmund. *The Church*. Contours of Christian Theology. Downers Grove, Ill.: InterVarsity Press, 1995. Evangelical Presbyterian.

Lubac, Henri de. *The Splendour of the Church*. Lanham, Md.: Sheed and Ward, 1956. Roman Catholic.

Moltmann, Jürgen. *The Church in the Power of the Spirit*. New York:

Harper, 1977. Reformed.

Pannenberg, Wolfhart. *The Church*. Philadelphia: Westminster Press, 1983). Lutheran.

Rahner, Karl. *The Church and the Sacraments*. St. Louis: Herder, 1963. Roman Catholic.

Williams, Rowan. *Anglican Identities*. Boston: Cowley Press, 2004. Anglican.

Advanced

Ratzinger, Joseph. *Called to Communion*. San Francisco: Ignatius, 1996. Roman Catholic.

Volf, Miroslav. *After Our Likeness*. Grand Rapids: Eerdmans, 1998. Evangelical.

Zizoulas, John. *Being as Communion*. Crestwood, N.Y.: St. Vladimir's Seminary Press, 1985. Orthodox.

Name and Subject Index

Scripture Index